AI OPTIONS TRADING FOR BEGINNERS

The Ultimate Guide to Leveraging AI to Generate Wealth with 50 Proven Strategies, Tactics, and Hacks to Minimize Risk, Maximize Profit, and Master the Market

Alex Bytes

1st Edition

ISBN: 978-3-69104-367-9
Lucid Page Media (an imprint of Orbita Media GmbH)
Ericusspitze 4
20457 Hamburg
Germany
contact@lucidpagemedia.com

TABLE OF CONTENTS

INTRODUCTION

1. Welcome to the Future of Trading

AI is no longer the future of trading—it's already the present. If you're still relying solely on traditional methods, you're falling behind. In the past, trading was dominated by human intuition and manual analysis, but today, technology is changing the game. Those who embrace this technological shift gain a real edge over traders still clinging to old-school techniques. If you have ever wondered how AI can enhance your trading decisions, minimize risk, and optimize profitability, this book will guide you through the transformation.

Trading options has long been regarded as a complex financial activity, requiring a deep understanding of market trends, risk management, and strategic execution. Traditionally, traders had to spend hours analyzing charts, reading financial reports, and following news that could impact market movements. With the rise of AI-driven tools, the barriers to entry are being lowered. Today, traders can leverage machine learning algorithms, predictive analytics, and automated systems to enhance their decision-making and execute trades with greater precision. AI enables traders to analyze vast data sets in seconds, spot hidden patterns, and make confident, data-driven decisions.

Traditional Trading

AI Trading

This book is designed to bridge the gap between traditional options trading and cutting-edge AI applications. Whether you are a complete beginner or a trader looking to refine your approach, the insights provided will help you harness AI to improve your strategies, reduce uncertainty, and ultimately maximize returns. You will learn the essential concepts of options trading, the role of AI in modern financial markets, and how to integrate AI-powered tools into your trading workflow.

2. Why This Book? What You Will Learn

The goal of this book is to provide a structured and practical approach to integrating AI into options trading. Unlike generic trading books that focus solely on theoretical concepts, this guide offers actionable insights, step-by-step strategies, and real-world applications. By the end of this book, you'll clearly understand how to apply AI to:

1. Analyze market data more effectively, uncovering trends and opportunities invisible to the human eye.

2. Automate your trading strategies, reducing the impact of emotional decision-making and human error.
3. Optimize entry and exit points, ensuring that you make the best trades at the right moments.
4. Mitigate risks through AI-driven models that assess market conditions and recommend adjustments.
5. Build a sustainable and profitable trading plan that balances risk and reward.

This isn't about empty promises or 'get-rich-quick' tricks. Instead, it focuses on equipping you with the knowledge and tools needed to trade intelligently, backed by data and AI-powered analysis. What sets this guide apart is its focus on real-world application—not just theory—so you can start trading smarter from day one.

3. The Rise of AI in Financial Markets

Artificial intelligence is revolutionizing every aspect of the financial world, from algorithmic trading in hedge funds to robo-advisors for retail investors. AI systems can analyze huge volumes of data in real time, spotting trends and market inefficiencies that a human would likely miss. Machine learning models can process historical data, recognize trends, and predict future movements with remarkable accuracy.

Major financial institutions and professional traders have been using AI for years, but recent advancements have made these technologies more accessible to independent traders. AI-powered platforms can now assist with risk management, trade execution, and portfolio optimization, leveling the playing field for those willing to embrace innovation.

As markets become increasingly volatile and unpredictable, relying solely on human intuition is no longer sufficient. AI helps traders cut emotional bias, boost efficiency, and rely on data-driven insights for better decision-making. Whether you are trading options, stocks, or other financial instruments, AI can give you a decisive edge in the market.

4. The Importance of Mastering Both AI and Options Trading

While AI can significantly enhance trading performance, it is not a substitute for foundational knowledge. Understanding options trading fundamentals is crucial before integrating AI-driven tools into your strategy. Many traders fall into the trap of blindly relying on AI without grasping the mechanics of the financial instruments they are dealing with. This often leads to poor decision-making and unnecessary losses.

A well-rounded trader leverages AI as a tool, not a crutch. The most successful market participants combine technical expertise with AI-enhanced analytics to create a comprehensive, adaptable approach. This book will provide both foundational knowledge of options trading and the practical implementation of AI to give you a competitive edge.

In the chapters ahead, you will learn how to integrate AI into your trading routine, develop automated strategies, and mitigate risks using AI-powered tools. By the end of this journey, you'll have the confidence and skills to trade options with precision and purpose.

The future of trading belongs to those who embrace technology. Are you ready to be one of them?

5. Who Is This Book For?

This book is tailored to a diverse range of readers who want to enhance their financial future using AI-driven options trading. Whether you're starting from scratch or aiming to sharpen your strategies with AI, this guide offers a clear, structured path forward.

Beginners with No Experience in Options Trading

If you have never traded options before, this book will serve as your step-by-step guide. It breaks down complex concepts into easy-to-understand explanations, ensuring that you build a strong foundation before integrating AI into your approach. You will learn everything from the basics of options contracts to advanced AI-powered risk management strategies.

Traders Looking to Integrate AI Into Their Strategies

If you are already familiar with options trading but want to take your skills to the next level, AI can be a game-changer. This book provides practical insights on how to leverage machine learning models, automate trade execution, and optimize decision-making. You will learn how AI can enhance market analysis, detect profitable opportunities, and minimize human errors in trading.

Those Seeking Financial Independence Through Smart Trading

Many traders enter the world of options trading with the goal of achieving financial independence. Whether you are looking to generate supplemental income, replace your primary job, or build long-term wealth, this book equips you with the tools needed to trade efficiently and strategically. AI-driven options trading offers a systematic approach to wealth accumulation while managing risk effectively.

Armed with the right knowledge and AI tools, anyone can become a skilled options trader. The key is to combine education, discipline, and technology to make informed trading decisions.

6. How to Use This Book

This book is structured to provide a logical and practical progression from the basics of options trading to advanced AI-driven strategies. Here's what you can expect:

The Structure of the Book and What to Expect

The book is divided into clear, progressive sections:

Part 1 lays the foundation of options trading, ensuring that even beginners can follow along.

Part 2 focuses on AI-powered trading strategies and risk management techniques.

Part 3 introduces automation tools and advanced strategies that can optimize your trading efficiency.

Actionable Strategies, Step-by-Step Guides, and Real-World Examples

Each chapter doesn't just explain the theory—it shows you how it works in real life. You will find case studies that illustrate successful AI-driven options trades, along with step-by-step walkthroughs of common trading strategies. Additionally, each chapter includes practical exercises designed to reinforce your learning and help you apply what you've learned directly in real-time trading.

The Mindset Shift Required for Trading Success

Options trading, particularly when integrating AI, requires a shift in mindset. Unlike traditional investing, which often relies on intuition and fundamental analysis, AI-powered trading is **data-driven** and requires discipline. You will learn how to:

1. Avoid common psychological traps, such as **fear-based** or **greedy** trading.
2. Develop a structured and systematic approach to trading using AI.
3. Maintain **risk management discipline** to protect your portfolio and maximize returns.

By following the structure of this book, you'll build not only the technical skills but also the right mindset to navigate the options market confidently and profitably.

PART 1:

THE FOUNDATIONS OF OPTIONS TRADING

CHAPTER 1: OPTIONS TRADING 101 – THE ESSENTIALS

Options trading is a powerful tool that offers traders flexibility, leverage, and effective ways to manage risk. Unlike traditional stock trading, where an investor buys and holds shares of a company, options allow traders to take strategic positions based on future price movements without having to own the underlying asset.

1. What Are Options?

This chapter covers the essential building blocks to get started with options trading—from what options are and how they work, to key terminology, to more advanced concepts like contract structures, market participants, and risk mitigation strategies.

The Difference Between Stocks and Options

Stocks and options serve different purposes in the financial markets. Stocks represent direct ownership in a company, granting shareholders voting rights and potential dividends. Options, on the other hand, are contracts that offer strategic benefits—like leverage and risk control—without full ownership of the asset. This distinction enables options traders to profit from price movements with far less capital than stock investors.

Feature	Stocks	Options
Ownership	Represents direct ownership in a company	A contract that provides rights, not ownership
Leverage	Requires full capital investment	Can control large positions with less capital
Risk Exposure	Direct exposure to market movements	Defined risk with predetermined maximum loss
Expiration	No expiration, held indefinitely	Limited lifespan with expiration date
Profit Potential	Gains depend on stock appreciation and dividends	Profits can be generated from movement in any direction

While both stocks and options are financial instruments traded in the market, they have fundamental differences:

Because options allow traders to control a large number of shares with relatively little capital, they provide opportunities for enhanced returns. However, leverage also amplifies risk—so it's essential to understand how options work before using them in any strategy.

How Options Work: Calls vs. Puts

There are two main types of options: call options and put options. A call option gives the holder the right to buy an asset at a set price before the expiration date, while a put option grants the right to sell at a predetermined price. Call options are used when traders expect the asset's price to rise, while put options are for when a drop is anticipated.

Example of a Call Option Trade

Imagine that Company XYZ is currently trading at $100 per share. You believe the stock will rise, so you buy a **call option** with a **strike price** of $110, expiring in one month, for a **premium** of $5 per share.

⇒ If the stock rises to **$120**, you can **exercise** your option to buy the stock at $110, selling it for a $10 gain per share—minus the $5 premium.

⇒ If the stock stays below $110, the option expires worthless, and you lose only the **$5 premium per share**.

Example of a Put Option Trade

Now, let's assume you own 100 shares of Company XYZ, currently trading at $100. You want to protect yourself from a potential decline, so you buy a **put option** with a strike price of $95, expiring in one month, for a **premium** of $3 per share.

⇒ If the stock falls to **$90**, you can exercise the put option to sell your shares at **$95**, avoiding further losses.

⇒ If the stock stays above **$95**, the put option expires worthless, and your maximum loss is the **$3 premium** per share.

Options offer flexibility to profit in both rising and falling markets—and can be used effectively for hedging.

Key Terminologies: Strike Price, Expiration, Premiums

Knowing the basic terms is key to placing successful trades:

⇒ **Strike Price**: The agreed-upon price at which the option can be exercised.

⇒ **Expiration Date**: The deadline by which the option must be exercised or it becomes worthless.

⇒ **Premium**: The cost of purchasing the option contract, which varies based on market conditions.

Other important terms include:

⇒ **Intrinsic Value**: The amount an option is "in the money."

⇒ **Extrinsic Value**: The portion of an option's price that comes from time value and volatility.

⇒ **Open Interest**: The total number of outstanding option contracts in the market.

⇒ **Bid-Ask Spread: The gap between what buyers want to pay and what sellers are asking.** By mastering these terms, traders can confidently navigate the options market.

The Role of Market Makers

Market makers keep the market liquid by always being ready to buy or sell at quoted prices. Their activity helps ensure smooth market function and tighter bid-ask spreads, benefiting retail traders.

2. Understanding Option Contracts

American vs. European Options

American options can be exercised at any time before expiration, while European options can only be exercised at expiration. This difference influences which strategies traders can use and how they manage risk.

What Happens at Expiration?

At expiration, options that are "in the money" may be exercised or settled for cash, while those "out of the money" expire worthless. Understanding expiration mechanics is key to managing risk effectively.

3. Why Trade Options?

Leverage and Capital Efficiency

Options let traders control large positions using only a fraction of the capital required to buy the stocks outright. Unlike purchasing stocks outright, where full payment is required, options enable traders to benefit from price movements while committing only a fraction of the total value. This leverage can amplify gains, but it also increases potential losses, making proper risk management essential.

Example of Leverage in Action

⇒ Buying 100 shares of a $50 stock = **$5,000 investment**

⇒ Buying a call option (costing $5 per share) controlling 100 shares = **$500 investment**

The potential **percentage return** on capital is significantly higher with options.

Risk Management Strategies

One of the key advantages of options trading is the ability to manage risk effectively. Traders can implement strategies like covered calls, protective puts, and spreads to hedge against losses and protect investments. These strategies help limit downside risk while still offering room for profit.

Options allow traders to manage risk effectively by employing various strategies. One common approach is the **Covered Call**, which involves selling call options against stocks already owned in order to generate income. Another is the **Protective Put**, where traders buy put options to hedge against potential declines in stock value. A more advanced strategy is the **Iron Condor**, used to profit from low volatility by simultaneously selling calls and puts at different strike prices.

These strategies help traders reduce risk while maintaining profitability.

Hedging Against Losses

Options are often used to hedge against negative price movements in the underlying asset. Investors who hold stocks can purchase put options as insurance against a decline in stock value. Similarly, businesses and institutional investors use options to hedge currency fluctuations, commodity prices, and interest rate risks, ensuring greater financial stability in volatile markets.

Options are widely used for hedging, allowing investors to protect their portfolios from unexpected market movements. For instance, a portfolio manager might buy put options on the S&P 500 to safeguard against a potential market downturn. Similarly, a commodity trader could use options to hedge against volatile oil prices. Meanwhile, a stock investor may choose to sell covered calls in order to generate extra income from existing holdings.

Hedging helps limit losses and provides greater stability in volatile markets.

4. Conclusion

This chapter introduced the fundamental principles of options trading, including how options work, key terminology, different contract types, and the reasons why traders use options.

The next chapter will delve deeper into advanced concepts like the Greeks, liquidity, and volatility, which are essential for optimizing risk management and maximizing profits in options trading.

Now that you understand how options work, you're ready to build more advanced strategies—and manage risk with more precision.

CHAPTER 2: THE CORE CONCEPTS OF OPTIONS TRADING

To trade options effectively, you need a solid grasp of a few key principles. While **Chapter 1** covered the basics of options trading, this chapter will focus on **risk management, pricing, and market dynamics**—critical components for any successful options trader.

You will learn about **the Greeks**, which measure different risk factors in options pricing, as well as **intrinsic and extrinsic value**, which determine an option's price. Finally, we will explore **liquidity and volatility**, two market factors that significantly impact the success of options strategies.

1. The Greeks – Risk Management in Options

Options pricing is complex because it is influenced by multiple variables, including time decay, price movement, and market volatility. The Greeks are risk metrics that help traders understand how various factors influence an option's price.

These risk factors include:

⇒ **Delta**: Sensitivity to price changes in the underlying asset.

⇒ **Gamma**: The rate of change of Delta.

⇒ **Theta**: The impact of time decay.

⇒ **Vega**: Sensitivity to implied volatility changes.

By mastering these metrics, traders can better predict option price movements and reduce risk exposure.

Understanding the Four Key Greeks

The Greeks are essential risk measures in options trading, providing insight into how an option's price will change in response to market factors.

- ⇒ **Delta** shows how much an option's price is likely to change with a $1 move in the underlying asset.
- ⇒ **Gamma** represents the rate of change of Delta, showing how Delta fluctuates as the price of the underlying asset shifts.
- ⇒ **Theta** measures time decay, or how much value an option loses each day as it nears expiration.
- ⇒ **Vega** gauges an option's sensitivity to changes in implied volatility, affecting the option's premium.

Understanding these Greeks enables traders to manage risk effectively and optimize their strategies.

DELTA: THE SENSITIVITY TO PRICE MOVEMENTS

Delta measures how much the price of an option is expected to change for every $1 move in the underlying asset.

For example, a call option with a Delta of 0.50 indicates that if the underlying stock rises by $1, the price of the option will increase by $0.50. Conversely, a put option with a Delta of -0.50 means that if the stock falls by $1, the value of the put option will rise by $0.50.

Using Delta in Trading

⇒ **High Delta options (0.70 - 1.00)** behave more like the stock itself.

⇒ **Low Delta options (0.10 - 0.30)** have a lower probability of finishing in the money but cost less.

Traders use Delta to estimate how their option's value might change with expected stock moves.

GAMMA: THE RATE OF CHANGE OF DELTA

Gamma measures how much **Delta** will change for every $1 move in the underlying stock.

Since Delta is not fixed, Gamma helps traders understand how quickly an option's price sensitivity changes.

For example, consider a call option that has a Delta of 0.50 and a Gamma of 0.05. If the underlying stock rises by $1, the Delta increases from 0.50 to 0.55, meaning the option becomes more sensitive to subsequent price movements.

Using Gamma in Trading

⇒ **High Gamma options** tend to experience larger price swings, making them suitable for traders expecting sharp price movements.

⇒ **Low Gamma options** are more stable and used for long-term strategies.

Traders watch Gamma closely when adjusting positions to hedge against sudden price moves.

THETA: THE EFFECT OF TIME DECAY

Theta measures how much an option's price will decrease as expiration approaches.

For example, an option with a Theta of -0.05 will lose $0.05 in value each day. As the expiration date approaches, this Theta decay accelerates, causing options to lose value more rapidly.

Using Theta in Trading

⇒ **Buyers of options** must be aware of time decay, as options lose value if the stock price doesn't move quickly enough.

⇒ **Option sellers** benefit from Theta, as they profit when options lose value and expire worthless.

This is why **option sellers** often profit from strategies like **covered calls and credit spreads**.

VEGA: THE IMPACT OF IMPLIED VOLATILITY

Vega measures an option's sensitivity to changes in market **volatility**.

For example, if an option has a Vega of 0.12 and the implied volatility increases by 1%, the price of the option will rise by $0.12. Conversely, if implied volatility decreases, the option's price will fall accordingly.

Using Vega in Trading

⇒ **High Vega options** become expensive in volatile markets.

⇒ **Low Vega options** perform better in stable market conditions.

Traders rely on Vega to manage volatility risk, especially around earnings reports or key market events.

How to Use the Greeks in Real Trades

1. **Delta Hedging**: Traders adjust their positions based on Delta values to neutralize market movement risk.
2. **Gamma Scalping**: Active traders use Gamma to fine-tune hedging strategies and maximize profitability in volatile markets.
3. **Theta Management**: Options traders monitor Theta to minimize time decay losses in long positions and capitalize on premium collection in short positions.
4. **Vega Strategies**: Traders use Vega to determine the impact of volatility on their options positions, particularly when trading earnings announcements or macroeconomic events.

Incorporating the Greeks into your strategy allows you to make smarter decisions and manage risk more effectively.

2. Intrinsic vs. Extrinsic Value

How to Evaluate Option Prices

An option's price is made up of two parts: intrinsic and extrinsic value. Intrinsic value is the portion of the option's price that comes from its relationship to the underlying asset's price. Extrinsic value, also known as time value, is the additional amount that traders are willing to pay due to factors such as time until expiration and market volatility.

Why Some Options Are More Expensive Than Others

Options with longer time until expiration tend to have higher extrinsic value due to the uncertainty of future price movements. Additionally, options on volatile stocks carry higher premiums because they have a greater likelihood of reaching profitable strike prices. Knowing how these two values interact helps traders decide which options to trade and when to enter or exit.

3. Liquidity & Volatility

How Market Conditions Affect Options Pricing

Conditions like supply and demand, trading volume, and macro events can strongly influence option prices. High volatility often leads to higher option premiums due to increased uncertainty, while low liquidity can widen bid-ask spreads, making it more expensive to enter and exit trades. Understanding these dynamics helps traders anticipate price movements and optimize their strategies.

How to Spot High-Liquidity Options for Better Trades

High-liquidity options are characterized by tight bid-ask spreads and high open interest, making them easier to trade without significant price slippage. Traders can identify liquid options by examining volume data, open interest, and the bid-ask spread. Choosing liquid options makes trading smoother and lowers costs, helping you maximize profits.

Here's how to spot the most liquid options:

1. **High Open Interest**: More contracts available = easier to buy/sell.
2. **Narrow Bid-Ask Spreads**: Less price difference between buyers and sellers.
3. **High Trading Volume**: Indicates active interest in the option.

Choosing **high-liquidity options** ensures **better trade execution and lower costs**.

4. Conclusion

This chapter covered essential **options trading concepts**, including **the Greeks, pricing, and market conditions**.

By mastering these principles, you'll be equipped to manage risk effectively, evaluate option pricing with confidence, and select trades that offer high liquidity.

In the next chapter, we'll explore how AI-powered strategies can take your options trading to the next level.

CHAPTER 3: AI IN TRADING – THE GAME CHANGER

The financial markets are rapidly evolving, and one of the most revolutionary changes in recent years has been the integration of artificial intelligence (AI) into trading. AI is transforming the way traders analyze markets, place trades, and manage risk. An industry once ruled by intuition and manual analysis is now driven by data, algorithms, and automation.

In this chapter, we will explore what AI is in trading, how it enables faster market analysis than humans, and the core technologies behind it, including machine learning, deep learning, and automation.

1. How AI Is Reshaping the Way We Trade

Artificial intelligence in trading refers to the use of algorithms, machine learning models, and automation to analyze market trends, execute trades, and optimize strategies. Unlike traditional trading, where traders rely on charts, indicators, and experience, AI-based trading leverages vast amounts of data to make objective, high-speed, and highly accurate trading decisions.

AI in trading operates in three key ways. First, it analyzes financial data—such as market trends, news, and earnings reports—much faster than any human could. Second, it predicts market movements by examining historical patterns and conducting sentiment analysis. Third, it automates trade execution using bots and algorithmic strategies. Thanks to these capabilities, AI helps traders eliminate emotional bias, improve efficiency, and make data-driven decisions that significantly reduce risk.

How AI Analyzes Markets Faster Than Humans

AI accelerates market analysis in several powerful ways. First, it processes vast volumes of data within seconds. AI-powered trading platforms can analyze stock prices, option chains, economic indicators like inflation, interest rates, and GDP reports, along with news sentiment from earnings announcements and press releases. They also monitor social media platforms such as Twitter, Reddit, and financial forums. For instance, hedge funds use AI to scan thousands of news sources instantly—an impossible task for human traders.

Second, AI identifies complex patterns in market data that often escape human observation. Through advanced technical analysis, it detects price trends, support and resistance levels, unusual volume spikes, and shifts in market sentiment. By examining historical data, it estimates the likelihood of future price movements with high precision.

Lastly, AI responds to market changes in real time. Unlike human traders who require time to process information and act, AI systems execute trades instantly based on predefined conditions. They dynamically adjust stop-loss levels according to volatility and detect anomalies fast enough to act before humans can react. A clear example is high-frequency trading (HFT), where AI-driven hedge funds execute thousands of trades per second based on live market conditions.

Machine Learning, Deep Learning, and Automation in Trading

AI-powered trading relies on three core technologies: machine learning, deep learning, and automation. Each contributes uniquely to enhancing accuracy and efficiency in the financial markets.

Machine learning forms the foundation of AI in trading. It allows systems to learn from historical market data and adapt based on real-time performance. These models analyze past trends, identify profitable patterns, and refine strategies over time. For instance, a machine learning algorithm might detect that a breakout is likely when the S&P 500 crosses its 50-day moving average on high volume—insight that traders can use to improve decision-making.

There are two main approaches within machine learning. In **supervised learning**, the model is trained on labeled data, such as historical stock prices and their outcomes. In contrast, **unsupervised learning** identifies hidden patterns in unlabeled data, making it ideal for discovering new trading strategies. As these models continue training on fresh data, their predictions become more accurate, and false signals are minimized.

Deep learning, a more advanced subset of machine learning, uses artificial neural networks to detect subtle, non-obvious relationships within large datasets. This technology goes beyond traditional indicators by recognizing complex market behaviors and processing unstructured data like financial news, earnings reports, and even CEO speech. For example, deep learning models can analyze millions of posts on Reddit or Twitter to detect shifts in investor sentiment before the broader market responds. Hedge funds have even used this technology to interpret the tone and language in CEO interviews to anticipate earnings outcomes. By merging multiple data sources, deep learning provides a comprehensive view of market dynamics—one that no human could match on their own.

Automation is what truly transforms AI into a game-changer. Rather than relying on manual trading, AI-powered bots can automate entire strategies. These systems monitor markets around the clock and execute trades the moment specific conditions are met. They also adjust stop-losses, take-profit levels, and hedging strategies dynamically in response to changing conditions.

There are several types of AI-driven automated trading. **Algorithmic trading** follows predefined rules to enter and exit positions. **High-frequency trading (HFT)** takes it further, executing thousands of trades per second to exploit micro-movements in price. **AI-powered portfolio management**, used by robo-advisors like Wealthfront and Betterment, continuously rebalances investment allocations based on risk profiles and market shifts, aiming to reduce risk while maximizing returns.

Conclusion

AI is transforming the world of trading by making market analysis significantly faster, smarter, and more precise. It processes data at speeds thousands of times greater than any human trader, enabling rapid and comprehensive evaluations of the market. Thanks to machine learning, AI continuously improves by recognizing patterns and adjusting based on experience. Deep learning takes this further by uncovering insights from sources like financial news, market sentiment, and global events—elements that traditional analysis often overlooks. Meanwhile, automation empowers AI-driven bots to operate around the clock, executing trades without the need for human intervention.

In the next section, we'll delve into how AI predicts market movements through tools like sentiment analysis, pattern recognition, and hedge fund strategies that involve backtesting AI-powered trading models.

2. How AI Predicts Market Movements

One of the most impactful uses of AI in trading is its ability to predict market movements with remarkable accuracy. Unlike human traders, who typically rely on past patterns, technical indicators, and news interpretation, AI can simultaneously process massive amounts of both structured and unstructured data. By combining sentiment analysis, pattern recognition, and backtesting, AI models are able to generate highly precise forecasts—offering traders a clear advantage.

In this section, we'll examine how AI evaluates market sentiment to understand trader psychology, detects price movements and technical patterns faster than any human could, and backtests strategies—much like hedge funds do—to enhance profitability.

Sentiment Analysis & Pattern Recognition

Market sentiment plays a crucial role in trading, as emotions such as fear, greed, uncertainty, and optimism often drive sudden price movements. AI can interpret this emotional landscape by analyzing millions of data points in real time, providing traders with valuable insights into the prevailing mood of the market.

Sentiment analysis is one of the most effective AI-driven techniques for gauging this mood. It works by examining a wide array of sources, including news articles, press releases, social media platforms like Twitter and Reddit, discussion forums, earnings call transcripts, CEO speech patterns, analyst reports, and investor sentiment surveys. By processing both textual and spoken content, AI can determine whether the overall sentiment surrounding a specific asset or the market in general is bullish, bearish, or neutral.

Take Tesla (TSLA) as an example. Ahead of an earnings announcement, traders might feel uncertain about what to expect. However, an AI model could detect rising optimism—such as an uptick in positive social media discussions, bullish analyst upgrades, and an increase in Google searches like "buying Tesla stock." These signals, taken together, indicate strong positive sentiment and may suggest that a price surge is likely.

Beyond analyzing sentiment, AI also excels at recognizing technical patterns more quickly and accurately than human traders. While traditional approaches rely on tools like moving averages, RSI, or Bollinger Bands, AI can simultaneously analyze thousands of price charts to identify key formations such as head and shoulders (which indicate trend reversals), breakout and breakdown patterns near critical support or resistance levels, mean reversion opportunities in overbought or oversold conditions, and volume-based signals that often suggest institutional buying or selling.

Consider a stock consolidating near a resistance level at $200. AI might recognize that, historically, 80% of stocks in similar setups rallied 10% within the following five days. If a spike in volume occurs, the AI confirms the breakout and initiates the trade—often before human traders have even reacted.

This ability to rapidly process vast amounts of data and identify high-probability setups gives AI-driven traders a substantial edge over those relying solely on manual analysis.

Backtesting with AI: How Hedge Funds Do It

Backtesting is a fundamental element of AI-powered trading strategies, enabling traders to evaluate the effectiveness of a strategy using historical market data—before putting real capital at risk. This process has long been used by hedge funds, which rely on machine learning simulations to optimize their trading models and reduce inefficiencies.

In essence, backtesting involves applying a trading strategy to past market scenarios to assess its performance. Key metrics include the win rate (the percentage of successful trades), maximum drawdown (the largest historical loss), the risk-reward ratio (the relationship between potential profits and losses), and the specific market conditions under which the strategy performs best. By simulating trades on historical data, traders can refine their strategies, discarding those that underperform before moving to live execution.

Hedge funds use AI-enhanced backtesting platforms capable of processing decades of historical data within minutes. These systems can automatically test thousands of variations of a given strategy and optimize risk management parameters to improve overall profitability.

Consider the example of a mean reversion strategy, where AI identifies stocks that have deviated significantly from their average price and anticipates a reversion. Through AI-powered backtesting, a hedge fund might examine 50 years of stock market data to uncover repeating patterns, evaluate how past market crashes impacted the strategy, and determine the most effective trading timeframe—be it daily, weekly, or even intraday. The AI could ultimately determine that a 4-hour timeframe yields the best profit-to-risk balance, allowing the fund to fine-tune the approach before deploying real capital.

However, backtesting alone isn't enough. To ensure that strategies remain effective in evolving market conditions, hedge funds also employ **walk-forward testing**. This technique addresses a critical issue: a strategy might perform well on historical data, but that doesn't guarantee future success. Walk-forward testing applies the strategy to new, unseen data to verify its adaptability.

For instance, imagine AI identifies a momentum strategy that delivered strong results from 2018 to 2020. When walk-forward testing is applied to 2021 data, the strategy falters. The AI adjusts the entry and exit parameters, as well as stop-loss rules, in response to changing volatility—resulting in significantly improved performance. This process helps hedge funds identify robust strategies that can withstand different market environments, reducing the risk of overfitting and focusing only on setups that demonstrate consistent reliability.

Conclusion

AI is revolutionizing trading by predicting market movements faster and more accurately than human traders.

⇒ Sentiment analysis captures real-time shifts in market psychology.

⇒ Pattern recognition finds technical setups before traders notice them.

⇒ Backtesting ensures strategies are profitable before risking real money.

⇒ Hedge funds use AI-powered simulations to optimize trading strategies.

In the next section, we will explore AI-powered tools and platforms that traders can use to apply these advanced techniques in real-world markets.

3. AI Tools for Options Trading

As artificial intelligence continues to reshape the financial industry, traders now have access to a variety of AI-powered tools that can optimize their strategies, enhance decision-making, and automate trade execution. Gone are the days of relying only on charts and gut feeling.

AI tools for options trading can be divided into two main categories. The first includes **AI-powered trading platforms**, which assist traders in market analysis, trade identification, and risk assessment. The second consists of **bots and algorithmic trading systems**, which automate the entire trading process, carrying out trades hands-free.

AI-Powered Trading Platforms

AI-powered trading platforms are designed to analyze financial markets in real time, identifying opportunities that traders might otherwise miss. These platforms process vast amounts of market data, detecting patterns, trends, and anomalies to provide actionable insights.

One of the most well-known AI-driven trading platforms is Trade Ideas, a software designed to scan the stock market for high-probability trades. Trade Ideas employs artificial intelligence to monitor price action, volume surges, and technical indicators, generating trade alerts that traders can review before execution. Unlike conventional screeners, which require manual configuration, Trade Ideas learns from historical data, constantly learning from data to deliver more accurate insights.

Another platform that has gained popularity is Tickeron, which specializes in AI-powered technical analysis. Tickeron identifies chart patterns such as head and shoulders formations, ascending triangles, and cup-and-handle setups with a high degree of precision. The AI evaluates the probability of success for each pattern, helping traders decide whether to enter or avoid a trade.

While these platforms provide insights, they do not execute trades automatically. They serve as intelligent assistants, enhancing traders' ability to analyze markets efficiently. For those seeking full automation, AI-driven trading bots and algorithmic trading systems offer a more hands-off approach.

Bots and Algorithmic Trading for Options

AI-driven bots and algorithmic trading systems have revolutionized options trading by automating the entire process, from market analysis to trade execution. These systems operate based on predefined rules and machine learning models, allowing traders to participate in the market without needing to monitor charts all day.

Algorithmic trading, also known as algo trading, involves the use of complex mathematical models to execute trades at optimal moments. These models consider multiple factors, such as market momentum, volatility levels, and order flow, to determine when to buy or sell an options contract. Unlike human traders, AI-driven algorithms react to market conditions instantly, ensuring that trades are executed with maximum efficiency.

One of the key advantages of AI-driven bots is their ability to eliminate emotional bias from trading. Many traders struggle with hesitation, overtrading, or exiting positions too soon due to fear or greed. AI bots stick to strict rules, ensuring that every trade adheres to a structured strategy.

For example, a trader using an AI options bot may configure the system to enter a trade only when specific conditions are met, such as implied volatility dropping below a certain level or an options contract experiencing an unusual spike in open interest. Once these conditions are satisfied, the bot executes the trade automatically, eliminating the need for manual intervention.

High-frequency trading (HFT) is another area where AI has had a profound impact. Hedge funds and institutional investors employ AI-powered algorithms to execute thousands of trades per second, capitalizing on tiny price discrepancies that human traders cannot detect. These sophisticated systems require advanced computing power and infrastructure, but similar technologies are now becoming more accessible to retail traders through cloud-based AI solutions.

Although AI-driven bots offer many benefits, they are not without risks. A poorly configured algorithm can lead to significant losses, especially if it fails to adapt to sudden market changes. AI-driven trading still requires regular monitoring to stay effective and fine-tune their systems to ensure they remain effective. Additionally, it is essential to have robust risk management protocols in place, such as stop-loss mechanisms and position-sizing rules, to prevent large drawdowns.

AI-powered tools are reshaping options trading by making market analysis more precise, execution more efficient, and strategies more disciplined. Whether through intelligent trading platforms that enhance decision-making or fully automated bots that execute trades with precision, artificial intelligence has become an indispensable tool for traders looking to gain an edge in the markets.

With AI continuing to evolve, the future of options trading will likely see even greater advancements, including self-learning algorithms that adapt in real time and predictive analytics capable of forecasting market moves with unprecedented accuracy. Those who embrace these tools will be best equipped to navigate the complexities of modern markets—and seize opportunities others miss.

PART 2: AI-POWERED OPTIONS TRADING STRATEGIES

CHAPTER 4: AI-POWERED ENTRY & EXIT STRATEGIES

The ability to enter and exit trades at the right moment is one of the most crucial skills in options trading. Even a solid trade idea can fall apart if the timing is wrong. Traditionally, traders have relied on technical indicators, chart patterns, and fundamental analysis to determine their entry and exit points. However, AI-powered strategies have dramatically improved this process, allowing traders to make data-driven decisions with greater accuracy and efficiency.

AI removes human bias from trading, eliminating emotional decision-making and ensuring that entry and exit points are based on statistical probabilities rather than intuition. By analyzing massive datasets, AI uncovers hidden trends, identify key support and resistance levels, and refine trade execution strategies.

This chapter explores how AI detects optimal entry points by analyzing trends and support/resistance zones, allowing traders to position themselves ahead of market movements with maximum precision.

1. How AI Detects Optimal Entry Points

An entry point in trading is the exact moment when a trader decides to open a position. Choosing the right entry point can mean the difference between a highly profitable trade and one that struggles to break even. Traditionally, traders identify entry points by using trend analysis, moving averages, candlestick patterns, and momentum indicators. While these methods have been effective, they come with limitations—human error, misinterpretation, and slow reaction times.

AI, on the other hand, processes millions of data points in real time, detecting high-probability entry signals with far greater accuracy than a human trader. Instead of relying on a few indicators, AI aggregates multiple factors simultaneously, providing a comprehensive analysis of the market.

Trend Analysis with AI

Trend analysis is a core component of entry strategy. Traditional traders use moving averages, trendlines, and price action to determine whether the market is in an uptrend, downtrend, or consolidation phase. AI takes trend analysis a step further by applying machine learning algorithms that dynamically adjust based on market conditions.

One of the ways AI enhances trend analysis is by identifying micro-trends within larger trends. While human traders typically see only broad movements, AI can detect smaller trend shifts that often precede major reversals or breakouts.

Example: AI Detecting a Trend Shift Before the Market Reacts

A trader analyzing the S&P 500 might interpret an uptrend based on the 50-day moving average, believing the market will continue to rise. However, AI can detect signs of weakening momentum earlier by evaluating factors such as declining volume during rallies, a shift in institutional order flow toward defensive assets, and divergences between leading stocks and the index itself. These early warnings allow AI-powered systems to adjust positions before a trend reversal occurs, helping to minimize losses and maximize potential gains.

Another key advantage of AI is its ability to identify false breakouts. Many traders fall into the trap of entering a position after a brief breakout above resistance, only to see the price reverse shortly afterward. AI mitigates this risk by analyzing historical breakout patterns and comparing them to current market conditions, determining whether a move is statistically likely to hold or fail.

By using AI for trend analysis, traders can eliminate much of the guesswork and adopt a more data-driven approach to market direction—ultimately improving the accuracy of their entries.

Using AI for Support & Resistance Identification

Support and resistance levels are fundamental concepts in technical analysis. They represent psychological price zones where buyers and sellers historically enter or exit positions. Identifying these levels manually, however, can be challenging—many traders misplace key levels or fail to recognize when old support turns into resistance.

AI-powered trading systems have revolutionized support and resistance analysis by scanning price history, order flow, and market structure to identify the most reliable price zones. Instead of relying on subjective trendlines, AI mathematically determines key areas based on historical reaction points, liquidity clusters, and volume distribution.

One of AI's most significant advantages is its ability to adjust dynamically as new data emerges. Traditional traders often rely on static support and resistance levels, but AI continuously updates these zones as market conditions evolve.

Example: AI Adapting Support & Resistance in Real Time

Imagine a stock that has repeatedly bounced near the $150 level, leading traditional traders to believe this area represents strong support. While this assumption may have held true in the past, AI takes a more nuanced approach. It detects that recent buying pressure at that level is fading, and large institutional sell orders are beginning to surface. Rather than relying on the idea that the support will hold, AI reevaluates the situation by analyzing changes in liquidity—such as an increase in large sell orders—alongside weakening momentum indicators and rising put option activity. Based on this updated information, it can adjust trade recommendations accordingly, helping traders avoid entering long positions at a level that's no longer reliable.

In addition, AI enhances support and resistance detection through volume profile analysis. Instead of drawing simple trendlines, it evaluates where significant trading activity has historically occurred, highlighting price levels with strong liquidity. This allows traders to better identify areas where institutions are accumulating or distributing shares, offering more precise and reliable entry points than conventional technical methods.

How AI Combines Trend & Support/Resistance for Superior Entries

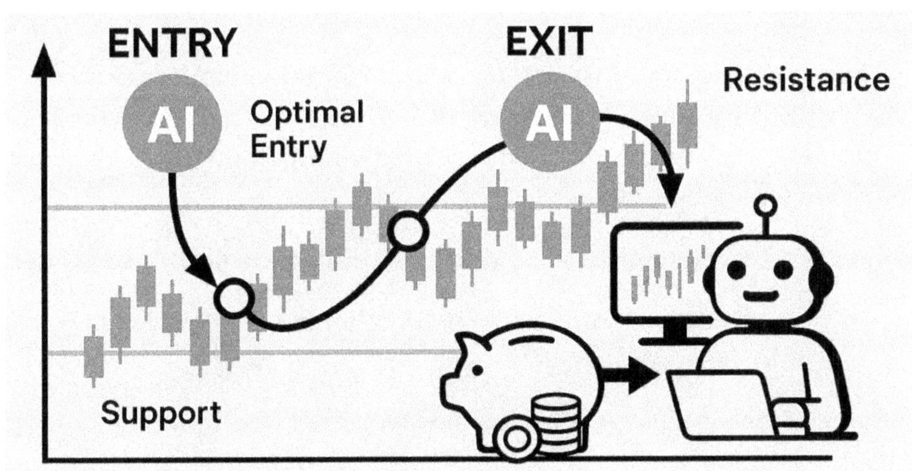

AI-powered entry strategies are most effective when trend analysis and support/resistance identification are combined. A trader may identify an uptrend using AI-generated signals, but the optimal entry point will be determined by waiting for price action to reach a statistically significant support zone.

For example, AI may detect that a stock is in a strong uptrend, but rather than entering at any random moment, it waits until the price:

1. Pulls back to a high-probability support level identified by volume clustering.

2. Shows an uptick in institutional buying activity detected through AI-based order flow analysis.

3. Aligns with a historical pattern where similar pullbacks led to rallies.

This multi-layered approach boosts the chances of a successful trade while reducing exposure to false signals. AI does not simply identify when to enter a trade—it refines the process by determining the most strategic and risk-efficient entry point.

Conclusion

AI has completely transformed how traders identify optimal entry points in the market. Traditional trend analysis and support/resistance methods, while still useful, are prone to human error and subjectivity. AI eliminates these limitations by:

- Processing millions of data points in real time to detect trends faster.

- Identifying support and resistance levels based on liquidity and order flow.

- Distinguishing between true breakouts and false moves.

By leveraging AI-powered strategies, traders can dramatically improve their entry timing, reducing the risks associated with poorly timed trades. Most importantly, AI offers a systematic, emotion-free way to trading that maximizes the probability of success.

In the next section, we will explore how AI automates exit strategies, ensuring that trades are closed at optimal levels to maximize profit and minimize risk.

2. Automating Exit Strategies

Identifying the right entry point is only half the equation in successful options trading. Just as crucial is knowing when to exit a trade, whether to secure profits or minimize losses. Traditional traders rely on static stop-losses and take-profit levels, but these methods are often ineffective in rapidly changing market conditions. Stop-losses are often triggered too early by market noise, while rigid profit targets may lead to missed opportunities for greater gains.

Artificial intelligence has transformed trade exit strategies by introducing dynamic, data-driven methods that adapt to market conditions in real time. AI-powered systems continuously analyze price action, volatility, and order flow to optimize when to close a position. This approach eliminates the guesswork and emotional decision-making that often lead traders to exit too early or hold onto losing trades for too long.

Stop-loss automation with AI

A stop-loss is designed to protect traders from excessive losses by automatically closing a position when the price reaches a predetermined level. While traditional stop-losses use fixed price points, AI-driven stop-loss mechanisms adjust dynamically based on market conditions. Rather than depending on a static level, AI continuously recalibrates stop-loss placement based on factors such as volatility, momentum shifts, and institutional order flow.

One way AI improves stop-loss execution is through volatility-based adjustments. Traditional stop-losses often fail because they do not account for natural price fluctuations. If an asset experiences high volatility, a fixed stop-loss may be triggered unnecessarily, taking the trader out of the position before the trend fully develops. AI addresses this by analyzing both historical and real-time volatility to determine an optimal stop-loss level that minimizes premature exits.

For example, if a stock typically fluctuates by two percent per day, an AI-driven stop-loss would place the exit threshold beyond that range, ensuring that normal price movements do not trigger an unnecessary loss. Conversely, if volatility drops, the AI reduces the stop-loss range to prevent unnecessary risk exposure.

AI also incorporates machine learning models that track institutional order flow. By analyzing real-time liquidity data, AI detects when large traders are entering or exiting positions. If the system identifies an increase in sell-side pressure from institutional players, it can proactively adjust the stop-loss to lock in profits before the trend reverses.

Another way AI automates stop-loss placement is by using pattern recognition. If the AI detects a formation that historically leads to trend reversals, such as a head-and-shoulders pattern or a bearish divergence on key indicators, it can automatically tighten the stop-loss to reduce downside risk. This approach allows traders to react to market shifts before they materialize into significant losses.

Using AI to Optimize Trailing Stops

Trailing stops are a widely used exit strategy that help traders lock in profits while still allowing room for a trade to grow. Unlike fixed stop-losses, which stay at a constant level, trailing stops move in the direction of a profitable trade, ensuring gains are protected if the trend reverses.

AI-powered trailing stops take this concept to the next level by dynamically adjusting the stop distance based on real-time market conditions. Rather than relying on a fixed percentage or dollar amount, these smart systems factor in momentum strength, volume trends, and order flow to fine-tune the exit point.

One major advantage of AI-driven trailing stops is their ability to adapt to changing market dynamics—especially accelerating trends. When an asset shows a surge in momentum, AI can widen the trailing stop to let the trade breathe, reducing the risk of getting stopped out prematurely. On the flip side, when momentum weakens, the system tightens the stop to secure profits before a potential reversal.

AI also enhances trailing stop placement by identifying key support and resistance levels. Instead of applying arbitrary trailing distances, the algorithm recognizes price zones where significant buying or selling activity has occurred in the past. For instance, if a stock nears a strong resistance level, AI might tighten the stop to protect profits in case of a rejection. If the trend remains strong with no clear resistance ahead, the system gives the trade more room to run.

Another advanced feature is the integration of options flow analysis. By tracking changes in open interest and institutional options activity, AI detects when large players are preparing for a potential reversal. For example, if big investors start loading up on put options during an uptrend, AI flags this as a warning and adjusts the trailing stop accordingly.

A practical use case for AI-powered trailing stops is earnings-related trading. Many traders aim to capitalize on post-earnings price movements but often exit too early due to uncertainty. AI can analyze historical earnings reactions and tailor the trailing strategy based on past volatility patterns. If a company's earnings typically lead to multi-day trends, the stop is widened to capture more upside. If the moves are usually short-lived, the stop is tightened to lock in profits before the momentum fades.

These smart trailing stops aren't just useful for single trades—they're also valuable in portfolio management. Hedge funds and institutional investors rely on AI-driven models to manage risk across multiple positions, continuously adjusting stops in response to changing market conditions. This kind of systematic approach helps minimize large drawdowns and improves long-term performance.

By automating exits with AI, traders gain a powerful edge in both risk management and profit optimization. Instead of making reactive decisions based on emotion, they benefit from precise, data-driven exits that align with real-time market behavior.

As markets grow more complex and volatile, AI-driven trade exits will become a must-have tool for traders who aim to stay consistently ahead.

CHAPTER 5: AI-ENHANCED LOW-RISK OPTIONS STRATEGIES

For beginners, options trading can feel overwhelming, especially with the complexity of advanced strategies. However, some options strategies are specifically designed to generate steady income with minimal risk. These approaches help traders gradually build experience, with a focus on preserving capital, managing risk, and aiming for consistent returns.

This chapter explores three of the best low-risk options strategies, explaining how AI enhances trade selection, execution, and adjustments to maximize efficiency while minimizing risk.

1. Covered Calls

Market Scenario

A trader owns **100 shares** of a stable, blue-chip stock and wants to generate additional income while maintaining long-term ownership. The stock is trading at **$50**, and the trader is willing to sell it at **$55** if the price rises.

Trade Setup

1. The trader **sells one call option** with a **$55 strike price** expiring in **one month**.
2. The premium received is **$2 per share**, generating **$200 in immediate income**.
3. If the stock remains below **$55**, the trader **keeps the shares and the premium**.

How AI Enhances Covered Calls

AI-powered platforms improve covered call strategies by:

⇒ Identifying **stocks with strong momentum and low volatility** for higher probability of profit.

⇒ Analyzing the **historical probability of options expiring worthless**, maximizing premium collection.

⇒ Selecting **optimal strike prices and expirations** using machine learning models.

⇒ Timing entry points based on **institutional buying patterns and implied volatility trends**.

For example, AI scans **thousands of stocks daily**, filtering out highly volatile stocks that increase the risk of early assignment. It also suggests the **best days to sell calls**, ensuring traders collect the highest premium while reducing downside risk.

Outcome Analysis

⇒ If the stock **stays below $55**, the trader **keeps the premium and can repeat the process next month**.

⇒ If the stock **rises above $55**, the shares are called away, but the trader profits from both the **premium and capital appreciation**.

⇒ AI also suggests when to roll or adjust positions, adapting to market shifts in real time.

2. Cash-Secured Puts

Market Scenario

A trader is interested in buying a stock at a lower price but wants to **earn income while waiting for the right entry point**. The stock is currently trading at **$60**, and the trader is comfortable buying it at **$55**.

Trade Setup

1. The trader **sells a $55 put option** expiring in **one month** and receives a **$3 premium**.
2. The trader sets aside **$5,500** in cash to buy 100 shares if assigned.
3. If the stock stays above **$55**, the trader **keeps the $300 premium** without buying shares.

How AI Enhances Cash-Secured Puts

AI enhances this approach by:

⇒ Scanning for **stocks with strong fundamentals and undervaluation signals**.

⇒ Calculating **optimal strike prices** based on probability models.

⇒ Detecting **elevated implied volatility**, ensuring the trader sells puts **when premiums are high**.

⇒ Adjusting position sizing using **AI-driven risk management algorithms**.

For instance, for example, AI may recommend selling puts during market pullbacks, ensuring traders buy shares **at discount prices** rather than overpaying in bullish conditions. AI also tracks **institutional put-buying activity**, confirming that smart money is accumulating shares at the same strike price.

Outcome Analysis

⇒ If the stock remains **above $55**, the put expires worthless, and the trader **keeps the $300 premium**.

⇒ If the stock **drops below $55**, the trader buys **100 shares at an effective price of $52** ($55 strike - $3 premium).

⇒ AI monitors market dynamics and can suggest rolling puts forward if the stock looks likely to fall further.

3. The Wheel Strategy

Market Scenario

A trader wants to **generate steady income while gradually building positions in quality stocks.** The Wheel Strategy combines **cash-secured puts and covered calls**, creating a **continuous income cycle**.

Trade Setup

STEP 1 – **Selling a Cash-Secured Put**

1. The trader sells a **$40 put** on a stock they want to own, collecting a **$2 premium**.
2. If the stock stays above **$40**, the put expires, and the trader **keeps the premium**.
3. If the stock **drops below $40**, the trader **buys 100 shares** at an effective price of **$38** ($40 - $2).

STEP 2 – **Selling a Covered Call**

1. After being assigned, the trader sells a **$45 covered call**, collecting another **$2 premium**.

2. If the stock remains **below $45**, the trader **keeps the premium and repeats the process**.

3. If the stock **rises above $45**, the shares are **sold at $45**, locking in **profits + premium income**.

The Wheel Strategy allows traders to **generate consistent income** while acquiring stocks at **discounted prices**.

<u>How AI Enhances the Wheel Strategy</u>

AI makes this strategy more effective by:

⇒ Selecting **stocks with steady long-term growth trends** to avoid volatility traps.

⇒ Timing **put sales during optimal volatility conditions** to maximize premiums.

⇒ Adjusting covered call strikes in real time to balance potential return and risk.

⇒ Preventing overexposure by **managing portfolio allocation** across multiple stocks.

For example, AI might suggest avoiding selling puts on stocks with **upcoming earnings**, reducing the risk of sudden price drops. It can also **adjust call strike prices** dynamically, locking in profits when the stock starts losing momentum.

Outcome Analysis

⇒ If the stock **never drops below the put strike**, the trader **continues collecting put premiums** every month.

⇒ If assigned shares, the trader **sells covered calls**, ensuring a **continuous cycle of income generation**.

⇒ AI optimizes **each phase of the strategy**, helping traders enter and exit at the most strategic moments.

Conclusion

For beginner traders, these three low-risk options strategies provide a structured approach to generating income without taking on excessive risk:

1. **Covered Calls** – Ideal for traders who already own shares and want to earn passive income by collecting premiums.
2. **Cash-Secured Puts** – Perfect for those looking to buy stocks at a discount while getting paid through option premiums.
3. **The Wheel Strategy** – A powerful, repeatable income cycle that combines selling puts and covered calls.

By mastering these foundational strategies—with the support of AI—you'll trade with confidence and clarity, following a defined plan instead of relying on hope.

In the next chapter, we'll explore 50 AI-enhanced trading strategies, taking your skills to the next level with advanced techniques that continue to prioritize risk management.

CHAPTER 6: 50 AI-ENHANCED STRATEGIES FOR OPTIONS TRADING

Options trading offers a broad spectrum of strategies tailored to different risk tolerances and financial goals. Traders use options not only to generate income, but also to hedge their portfolios or speculate on market movements. Some strategies are well-suited for conservative investors seeking steady returns, while others are designed for more aggressive traders pursuing higher rewards.

Today, AI tools are transforming how these strategies are implemented. By enhancing trade selection, managing risk in real time, and optimizing entry and exit points, AI-driven models can analyze trends, detect market inefficiencies, and execute trades with a level of precision that far exceeds human capability.

To simplify the learning curve, this chapter organizes the 50 strategies into three sections, grouped by risk level—from low to high. We begin with low-risk approaches, ideal for beginners who want consistent returns with minimal downside.

There's no need to master all 50 strategies at once. Each one is crafted for specific market conditions and risk profiles. Within these pages, you'll find strategies focused on income generation, volatility plays, hedging, and more. Start with the ones that align best with your current goals and experience level—then build your toolkit as you grow.

1. AI-Powered Trend Trading Strategies

Strategy 1: AI Momentum Trading

Market Scenario

A stock has been on a strong upward trend for several weeks, showing increasing volume and breaking resistance levels. Traditional momentum indicators like RSI and MACD confirm the uptrend, but AI models suggest an even stronger continuation based on historical data.

Trade Setup

To capitalize on this momentum, the trader buys a **deep in-the-money call option** with a strike price slightly below the current stock price. Suppose the stock is trading at **$150**, and AI models predict a move to **$160** in the next two weeks.

1. Buy **$145 strike call option** expiring in **two weeks** at **$7.50 premium**.
2. The breakeven price is **$152.50** (strike + premium).

AI Enhancement

AI scans thousands of past momentum setups to determine the optimal entry point, avoiding false breakouts. The system monitors unusual trading volume and institutional order flows, increasing the probability of a strong price move.

Outcome Analysis

a) If the stock reaches **$160**, the option is worth at least **$15** (profit of **$7.50 per contract**).

b) If the stock stays at **$150**, the trade breaks even due to time decay.

c) If the stock drops below **$145**, the maximum risk is the premium paid.

Strategy 2: AI Volatility Breakout

Market Scenario

A biotech company is awaiting FDA approval for a new drug, with an announcement expected next week. Historically, similar stocks have seen volatility spikes post-announcement, making it a high-probability breakout scenario.

Trade Setup

The trader executes a **long straddle**, expecting a large move in either direction:

1. Buy **$80 strike call option** expiring in **one week** for **$5.20**.
2. Buy **$80 strike put option** expiring in **one week** for **$4.80**.
3. Total premium paid: **$10 per share**.

AI Enhancement

AI analyzes past biotech stock reactions to FDA announcements, identifying historical breakout patterns. It also scans social media sentiment and options flow to gauge whether implied volatility is underpriced or overpriced.

Outcome Analysis

a) If the stock moves **above $90** or **below $70**, one leg of the straddle profits significantly.

b) If the stock remains flat, implied volatility collapse results in a loss.

c) AI suggests adjustments post-announcement if volatility remains high.

Strategy 3: Fibonacci and AI Pattern Matching

Market Scenario

A tech stock is in a retracement phase after a strong uptrend. AI identifies a **61.8% Fibonacci retracement level** that historically leads to reversals in this stock.

Trade Setup

The trader executes a **bullish call spread** in anticipation of a reversal. If the stock is trading at **$120**, and AI predicts a bounce from **$115**, the trader:

1. Buys a **$115 strike call option** expiring in **three weeks** for **$6.00**.
2. Sells a **$125 strike call option** expiring in **three weeks** for **$2.50**.
3. Total cost: **$3.50 per share**.

AI Enhancement

AI scans past retracements in similar market conditions, identifying the highest probability reversal points. The system continuously adjusts risk parameters, suggesting stop-loss levels if the setup fails.

Outcome Analysis

a) If the stock rebounds to **$125**, the spread reaches full profit (**$10 – $3.50 = $6.50 per share**).

b) If the stock remains at **$115**, the max loss is the premium paid (**$3.50 per share**).

c) AI suggests rolling the trade if new bullish signals emerge.

2. Volatility-Based Strategies

Strategy 4: AI-Based Earnings Straddle

Market Scenario

Company XYZ is reporting earnings tomorrow. AI detects a historically high probability of post-earnings volatility exceeding implied volatility expectations.

Trade Setup

To profit from a large price swing, the trader enters a **straddle** with:

1. Buy **$100 strike call** expiring in **one week** for **$4.50**.
2. Buy **$100 strike put** expiring in **one week** for **$4.20**.
3. Total cost: **$8.70 per share**.

AI Enhancement

AI analyzes past earnings reactions, institutional sentiment, and implied volatility mispricing to confirm the trade. It monitors real-time order flow and suggests closing early if pre-earnings volatility expands.

Outcome Analysis

a) If the stock moves above **$110** or below **$90**, the trade is highly profitable.

b) If the stock remains near **$100**, implied volatility crush results in a loss.

c) AI provides exit alerts based on post-earnings volatility conditions.

Strategy 5: AI Market Sentiment Strangle

Market Scenario

AI scans financial news and detects a major shift in sentiment for a stock due to regulatory changes.

Trade Setup

A trader sets up a **strangle**, expecting an outsized move in either direction:

1. Buy **$95 strike put** expiring in **two weeks** for **$3.50**.
2. Buy **$105 strike call** expiring in **two weeks** for **$3.20**.
3. Total cost: **$6.70 per share**.

AI Enhancement

AI scans **Twitter, Reddit, and financial news sentiment** to detect real-time public perception shifts. It suggests whether to hold, roll, or exit based on continued volatility expectations.

Outcome Analysis

a) If the stock moves above **$110** or below **$90**, the trade profits.

b) If the stock stays near **$100**, implied volatility collapse results in a loss.

c) AI continuously monitors news updates to adjust position sizing dynamically.

3. Risk Management and Hedging Strategies

Strategy 6: Dynamic AI Hedging

Market Scenario

A trader holds a portfolio of tech stocks and wants to protect against a potential downturn without completely exiting positions. AI detects a rise in implied volatility and an increase in downside risk indicators, suggesting that a hedge is necessary.

Trade Setup

The trader uses AI to optimize a protective put strategy:

1. Buy **$300 strike put option** expiring in **one month** for **$12.50.**
2. AI suggests adjusting the strike and expiration dynamically based on changing volatility conditions.

AI Enhancement

AI continuously tracks **market volatility, macroeconomic data, and institutional order flow**, adjusting the hedge dynamically. If risk decreases, AI might suggest rolling the put to a lower strike price, reducing costs.

Outcome Analysis

a) If the portfolio declines, the put option increases in value, offsetting losses.

b) If the market stabilizes, AI suggests reducing hedge exposure.

c) The AI prevents over-hedging, ensuring that the trader doesn't waste capital on unnecessary protection.

Strategy 7: AI-Powered Protective Collar Strategy

Market Scenario

A trader owns 1,000 shares of a stock trading at **$150**. AI detects potential downside risk but suggests using a **collar strategy** instead of selling the stock outright.

Trade Setup

1. Buy **$140 put option** expiring in **two months** for **$4.00**.
2. Sell **$160 call option** expiring in **two months** for **$4.50**.
3. The net credit is **$0.50 per share**, reducing downside risk while allowing moderate upside gains.

AI Enhancement

AI determines the optimal strike price for **maximum downside protection at minimal cost**. It tracks implied volatility to adjust the hedge dynamically.

Outcome Analysis

a) If the stock falls to **$140**, the put offsets losses.

b) If the stock rises above **$160**, the covered call is exercised, locking in gains.

c) AI helps balance risk and profit potential efficiently.

Strategy 8: AI-Driven Risk Reversal

Market Scenario

A stock is experiencing high bearish sentiment, but AI detects that the negativity is **overdone** based on historical data. Instead of buying calls outright, a trader executes a **risk reversal** strategy.

Trade Setup

1. Sell **$80 strike put** expiring in **one month** for **$3.00**.
2. Buy **$90 strike call** expiring in **one month** for **$3.00**.
3. The trade has **zero cost**, using the premium collected from the put to fund the call purchase.

AI Enhancement

AI models predict **mean reversion**, detecting that **market pessimism is exaggerated**. AI also tracks institutional order flow to confirm whether big players are positioning for a reversal.

Outcome Analysis

a) If the stock rebounds, the **call option profits significantly** while the put expires worthless.

b) If the stock falls, the trader **must buy the stock at $80**, but AI adjusts hedge levels dynamically.

Strategy 9: Rolling Covered Calls with AI

Market Scenario

A trader holds 500 shares of a dividend-paying stock. AI detects **a temporary price stall**, making it a great time to sell covered calls for additional income.

Trade Setup

1. Sell **$60 strike call option** expiring in **three weeks** for **$2.00 premium**.
2. AI monitors implied volatility, suggesting when to roll the position forward for **maximum yield**.

AI Enhancement

AI analyzes **historical premium decay, dividend schedules, and open interest** to suggest rolling covered calls at the optimal time.

Outcome Analysis

a) If the stock remains under **$60**, the trader **keeps the premium and can roll to another call**.

b) If the stock rises above **$60**, the shares are called away, but the trader earns from price appreciation and premium collection.

4. Income Generation Strategies

Strategy 10: AI-Based Wheel Strategy

Market Scenario

A trader wants to **generate passive income** by selling puts and covered calls on fundamentally strong stocks. AI helps optimize entry timing.

Trade Setup

1. Sell **$95 strike put option** expiring in **one month** for **$4.00**.
2. If assigned, AI suggests selling **$105 covered call** for additional income.

AI Enhancement

AI evaluates **historical win rates, market trends, and volatility** to suggest the best stocks for the wheel strategy. It also detects optimal times to roll positions for increased premium collection.

Outcome Analysis

a) If the put expires worthless, the trader **keeps the premium**.

b) If assigned, AI optimizes covered call sales for additional profit.

Strategy 11: Automated Cash-Secured Puts

Market Scenario

A trader wants to buy a stock but **only at a lower price** while earning premium income. AI selects high-probability put-selling opportunities.

Trade Setup

2. If assigned, buy the stock at an effective cost of **$47**.

1. Sell **$50 strike put** expiring in **one month** for **$3.00 premium**.
2. If assigned, buy the stock at an effective cost of **$47**.

AI Enhancement

AI detects stocks with **strong support levels** and selects strike prices that maximize premium collection while reducing downside risk.

Outcome Analysis

a) If the stock stays above **$50**, the trader **keeps the $3.00 premium**.

b) If the stock drops below **$50**, the trader buys the stock at a discount and can then sell covered calls.

Strategy 12: AI-Based Dividend Capture Using Options

Market Scenario

A stock with a **4% annual dividend yield** is about to go ex-dividend. AI suggests a strategy to **capture the dividend** while hedging against stock price fluctuations.

Trade Setup

1. Buy **100 shares** of the stock.
2. Sell **$110 covered call** expiring after the ex-dividend date for **$2.50 premium**.
3. The trader receives both the dividend and the premium.

AI Enhancement

AI identifies **historically stable dividend-paying stocks** and tracks option premiums to determine the best **call strikes** that allow dividend collection without excessive assignment risk.

Outcome Analysis

a) If the stock remains below **$110**, the trader **keeps the premium and the dividend**.

b) If the stock rises above **$110**, the trader is assigned but **still profits from premium, dividend, and stock appreciation**.

5. AI-Based Algorithmic Trading for Options

Strategy 13: AI-Powered Market Making

Market Scenario

Market makers provide liquidity by continuously quoting buy and sell prices for options contracts. A trader wants to leverage AI to act as a **mini-market maker**, capturing bid-ask spreads efficiently.

Trade Setup

1. AI identifies **high-liquidity options** with tight bid-ask spreads.
2. The trader simultaneously places **limit orders to buy options at the bid price and sell at the ask price**.
3. AI continuously adjusts quotes based on volatility and order flow.

AI Enhancement

AI tracks **institutional order flow, volatility shifts, and market depth** to adjust spreads dynamically, ensuring optimal execution.

Outcome Analysis

a) If spreads widen, the AI **adjusts quotes automatically to avoid losses**.

b) If liquidity dries up, AI **temporarily exits and re-enters when conditions improve**.

Strategy 14: AI-Based Order Flow Analysis

Market Scenario

Institutional traders often place large block orders, creating opportunities for retail traders who can spot the activity early. AI detects these moves by analyzing unusual volume spikes.

Trade Setup

1. AI scans options flow for **large call or put purchases**, indicating directional bias.
2. If AI detects a surge in **bullish call buying**, the trader buys **out-of-the-money call options** with a short expiration.

AI Enhancement

AI filters **false signals**, ensuring that only **high-probability institutional trades** are followed.

Outcome Analysis

a) If the institution is right, the option appreciates quickly.

b) AI suggests early exits if order flow reverses.

Strategy 15: High-Frequency Options Trading with AI

Market Scenario

A trader wants to **capitalize on microsecond price inefficiencies** in the options market. Traditional retail traders cannot execute at high speed, but AI-driven bots can.

Trade Setup

1. AI continuously scans bid-ask spreads, **placing limit orders milliseconds ahead of competitors**.
2. The bot **executes multiple trades per second**, profiting from rapid price movements.

AI Enhancement

AI models **predict short-term price fluctuations**, allowing the trader to profit from rapid market swings.

Outcome Analysis

a) If market conditions are stable, the bot profits consistently.

b) AI prevents overtrading, **pausing execution during high volatility spikes**.

Strategy 16: AI-Powered Liquidity Arbitrage

Market Scenario

A trader notices that the **same options contract is priced differently across exchanges** due to temporary liquidity imbalances. AI identifies these arbitrage opportunities.

Trade Setup

1. AI finds an options contract priced **$1.50 on one exchange** and **$1.30 on another**.

2. The trader simultaneously buys on the **cheaper exchange** and sells on the **higher-priced exchange**.

AI Enhancement

AI monitors liquidity across multiple markets in **real-time**, executing arbitrage trades instantly.

Outcome Analysis

a) If pricing normalizes, the trader captures **risk-free profit**.

b) AI prevents execution when fees make the trade unprofitable.

6. Multi-Leg Option Strategies Optimized by AI

Strategy 17: Iron Butterfly with AI Optimization

Market Scenario

A trader expects **low volatility** in a stock, making an **iron butterfly** a good choice. AI suggests the best strike prices based on historical price ranges.

Trade Setup

1. Sell **$100 strike call** and **$100 strike put**.
2. Buy **$95 put** and **$105 call** to define risk.

AI Enhancement

AI tracks **implied volatility**, ensuring the iron butterfly is placed **when option premiums are high**.

Outcome Analysis

a) If the stock stays at **$100**, the trade reaches **maximum profit**.

b) If volatility increases unexpectedly, AI suggests adjustments.

Strategy 18: Condor Variations (Broken-Wing, Ratio Spread)

Market Scenario

A stock is expected to trade within a defined range, but AI detects a **slight bullish bias**. The trader modifies a standard iron condor into a **broken-wing condor** for additional upside potential.

Trade Setup

1. Sell **$100 put** and buy **$95 put**.
2. Sell **$110 call** and buy **$120 call**.
3. AI adjusts the condor structure based on volatility conditions.

AI Enhancement

AI optimizes **spread width, expiration selection, and strike price adjustments** to ensure **higher profit potential**.

Outcome Analysis

a) If the stock stays within range, the condor profits.

b) If the stock breaks out, AI suggests adjustments.

Strategy 19: Reverse Iron Condor for Volatility Surges

Market Scenario

AI predicts **an upcoming volatility explosion** based on unusual options activity, making a **reverse iron condor** a suitable trade.

Trade Setup

1. Buy **$95 put** and sell **$100 put**.
2. Buy **$105 call** and sell **$110 call**.
3. The position profits from **large moves in either direction**.

AI Enhancement

AI detects **pre-volatility spikes**, ensuring entry **before implied volatility increases**.

Outcome Analysis

a) If volatility increases, the trade profits from expansion in option premiums.

b) AI monitors real-time volatility, adjusting the position if needed.

Strategy 20: AI-Driven Calendar Spreads

Market Scenario

A trader wants to profit from **time decay** while expecting minimal price movement. AI suggests the optimal stock and expiration date for a **calendar spread**.

Trade Setup

1. Sell **one-month $100 call** for **$4.00**.
2. Buy **three-month $100 call** for **$6.50**.
3. AI suggests rolling the front-month option to maximize theta decay.

AI Enhancement

AI **tracks historical volatility cycles**, suggesting **when to enter and roll the trade** for maximum profit.

Outcome Analysis

a) If the stock remains around **$100**, the spread profits from time decay.

b) AI provides alerts when implied volatility shifts, suggesting early exits if needed.

7. AI-Powered Short-Term Trading (Scalping & Day Trading)

Strategy 21: AI-Based Scalping with Options

Market Scenario

A trader wants to **capitalize on small price fluctuations** in a highly liquid stock. AI identifies **short-term momentum shifts** and executes trades automatically.

Trade Setup

1. AI detects rapid **bid-ask spread contractions**, signaling a short-term breakout.
2. The trader **buys at-the-money call options** with a **one-day expiration**.
3. AI monitors order flow to **exit within minutes**, locking in small gains.

AI Enhancement

AI-driven scalping **filters false breakouts**, ensuring only **high-probability trades** are executed.

Outcome Analysis

a) If momentum continues, the **scalping bot executes multiple trades**, compounding small profits.

b) If momentum fades, AI **cuts losses instantly**, minimizing drawdowns.

Strategy 22: AI Real-Time Arbitrage Detection

Market Scenario

A trader wants to **exploit temporary mispricings** in options premiums due to high-frequency order imbalances.

Trade Setup

1. AI scans options chains for **mispriced contracts** across exchanges.
2. It places simultaneous **buy and sell orders** to capture price inefficiencies.

AI Enhancement

AI executes arbitrage **faster than human traders**, ensuring the trade is profitable before price corrections occur.

Outcome Analysis

a) If the inefficiency persists, the trade yields **risk-free profits**.

b) AI prevents execution if bid-ask spreads **suddenly widen**, avoiding losses.

Strategy 23: Flash Crash Protection via AI Hedging

Market Scenario

A trader holds a long options position, but AI detects **market instability** that could lead to a flash crash.

Trade Setup

- AI **automatically buys deep out-of-the-money puts** to hedge against a sudden drop.
- AI monitors **real-time order flow imbalances** to suggest adjustments.

AI Enhancement

AI **detects early warning signals** of market crashes by analyzing high-frequency trading data.

Outcome Analysis

a) If a flash crash occurs, the **puts spike in value**, offsetting portfolio losses.

b) If the market stabilizes, AI **suggests exiting the hedge** at minimal cost.

Strategy 24: AI-Driven Real-Time Option Flow Analysis

Market Scenario

A trader wants to **track large institutional options orders** to predict future price moves.

Trade Setup

1. AI identifies **unusual options activity**, such as **large call buys** on a stock with no news.
2. The trader **buys call options** alongside the institutional flow, anticipating a price move.

AI Enhancement

AI filters **false signals**, ensuring only **high-confidence institutional trades** are tracked.

Outcome Analysis

a) If institutions are correct, the **options gain rapidly** as price follows order flow.

b) AI suggests an **early exit** if sentiment changes.

8. Deep Learning & AI-Based Fundamental Strategies

Strategy 25: AI-Based Earnings Prediction & Option Play

Market Scenario

Company XYZ is about to report earnings. AI predicts a **higher-than-expected** earnings beat.

Trade Setup

1. AI suggests a **bullish call spread** to capitalize on the anticipated move.
2. Buy **$100 strike call** expiring **one month post-earnings**.
3. Sell **$110 call** to reduce cost.

AI Enhancement

AI analyzes **earnings transcripts, sentiment analysis, and historical earnings patterns** to predict the probability of a positive surprise.

Outcome Analysis

a) If earnings exceed expectations, the **call spread profits** from post-earnings stock rally.

b) If earnings disappoint, AI **suggests hedging before volatility collapses**.

Strategy 26: AI-Based Insider Trading Signal Interpretation

Market Scenario

AI detects **unusual insider buying** in a stock, signaling **confidence from executives**.

Trade Setup

1. AI suggests **buying long-dated call options** to ride insider-driven moves.
2. Buy **six-month $50 strike call options** with **moderate leverage**.

AI Enhancement

AI tracks **SEC filings, insider transactions, and historical insider trading effects** on stock prices.

Outcome Analysis

a) If insiders are correct, the **stock rallies**, and the calls appreciate.

b) AI monitors **unusual selling activity**, suggesting an early exit if necessary.

Strategy 27: NLP (Natural Language Processing) for Market Sentiment

Market Scenario

AI scans financial news, social media, and earnings transcripts to **detect sentiment shifts**.

Trade Setup

1. If AI detects a sudden **positive sentiment shift**, buy a **short-term call option**.
2. If sentiment turns bearish, **buy puts** before the broader market reacts.

AI Enhancement

NLP-powered AI analyzes **thousands of data points**, detecting shifts **before human traders**.

Outcome Analysis

a) If sentiment continues trending in AI's predicted direction, **options gain rapidly**.

b) AI suggests exits if sentiment **reverses unexpectedly**.

Strategy 28: Neural Network-Driven Options Pricing

Market Scenario

Traditional Black-Scholes models **fail to price options accurately** in high-volatility markets. AI provides more precise pricing.

Trade Setup

AI suggests **buying underpriced options** and **selling overpriced ones**, based on deep learning models.

AI Enhancement

Neural networks analyze **implied volatility patterns, real-time demand, and historical mispricings**.

Outcome Analysis

a) If AI's pricing model is correct, **options converge to their true value**, generating profit.

b) AI continuously updates pricing forecasts, suggesting new opportunities.

9. Advanced AI & Automation Strategies

Strategy 29: AI-Based Dynamic Hedging with Automated Adjustments

Market Scenario

A trader holds multiple open options positions, but AI detects a **sudden volatility shift**.

Trade Setup

AI **automatically hedges the portfolio** by buying **adjusted put or call spreads**.

AI Enhancement

AI dynamically adjusts hedging positions **based on real-time risk factors**.

Outcome Analysis

a) If market conditions worsen, **AI-adjusted hedges prevent major losses**.

b) If conditions improve, AI **removes excess hedging** to preserve capital.

Strategy 30: AI-Driven Gamma Scalping for Market Makers

Market Scenario

A trader wants to **profit from gamma fluctuations** in a volatile market.

Trade Setup

AI suggests adjusting **delta-neutral positions** dynamically to capture gamma movement.

AI Enhancement

AI **monitors implied volatility shifts** and suggests optimal scalping adjustments.

Outcome Analysis

a) If gamma exposure increases, AI **executes profitable adjustments** automatically.

b) AI prevents excessive rebalancing, avoiding unnecessary trade commissions.

10. Advanced AI & Automation Strategies

Strategy 31: AI-Based Market Manipulation Detection

Market Scenario

A trader wants to avoid being trapped by **institutional order manipulation** and **high-frequency trading (HFT) tricks**. AI helps detect suspicious patterns.

Trade Setup

1. AI scans **real-time order book activity**, identifying large orders placed and canceled instantly (spoofing).
2. If AI detects manipulation, it suggests **avoiding trades or taking contrarian positions**.

AI Enhancement

AI tracks **anomalies in bid-ask spreads, volume spikes, and HFT behaviors**, alerting traders to manipulation risks.

Outcome Analysis

a) If manipulation is detected, traders **avoid losses by staying out of the trade**.

b) If the AI finds an **exploitable pattern**, it suggests profitable countertrades.

Strategy 32: AI & Quantum Computing for Options Trading

Market Scenario

A hedge fund seeks an **edge in high-speed options trading**, leveraging AI-powered quantum computing to analyze **millions of scenarios per second**.

Trade Setup

1. Quantum AI analyzes **historical market conditions** and **simulates thousands of potential trade outcomes instantly**.
2. The system selects the **highest probability trades** based on complex pattern recognition.

AI Enhancement

Quantum computing **removes computational bottlenecks**, making AI-powered predictions **more accurate and faster** than traditional models.

Outcome Analysis

a) If successful, **traders consistently enter high-probability positions**.

b) AI adjusts trades in real-time **as market conditions shift**.

Strategy 33: Fully Automated AI Portfolio with Options Strategies

Market Scenario

A trader wants a **fully hands-off approach**, allowing AI to execute all **options strategies, risk management, and adjustments**.

Trade Setup

1. AI builds and manages an options portfolio using a **mix of credit spreads, covered calls, and hedging strategies**.
2. AI dynamically reallocates positions based on changing market trends.

AI Enhancement

AI **continuously scans for profitable opportunities**, executing trades automatically while following strict risk parameters.

Outcome Analysis

a) If market conditions change, AI **adjusts the portfolio instantly**.

b) If volatility spikes, AI increases **hedging measures** automatically.

11. AI-Powered Risk Reduction & Portfolio Optimization Strategies

Strategy 34: AI-Based Volatility Skew Arbitrage

Market Scenario

A trader notices that **some options contracts have unusually high implied volatility**, making them overpriced relative to historical data.

Trade Setup

1. AI identifies mispriced **out-of-the-money put or call options** with extreme implied volatility skews.
2. The trader **sells overpriced options and buys underpriced ones** to capture the inefficiency.

AI Enhancement

AI monitors **historical volatility patterns, tracking when skew anomalies create profitable arbitrage opportunities**.

Outcome Analysis

a) If volatility normalizes, **the trader profits from the pricing correction**.

b) AI prevents execution if **skew remains artificially inflated**, avoiding false signals.

Strategy 35: AI-Enhanced Monte Carlo Simulations for Options Pricing

Market Scenario

Traditional pricing models like Black-Scholes **fail in high-volatility environments**. AI-powered Monte Carlo simulations provide **more accurate pricing predictions**.

Trade Setup

1. AI runs **thousands of simulations** on different market scenarios, optimizing entry and exit prices.
2. AI suggests the best trade **based on probability-weighted outcomes**.

AI Enhancement

Monte Carlo AI integrates **real-time market shifts**, making pricing models more **adaptive to current volatility conditions**.

Outcome Analysis

a) If AI's predicted price range holds, **the trader consistently profits from superior trade selection**.

b) If conditions shift unexpectedly, AI **adjusts probability weightings and suggests alternative trades**.

Strategy 36: AI-Driven Smart Portfolio Rebalancing with Options

Market Scenario

A long-term investor wants to **hedge portfolio risk while maintaining a balance of income generation and growth**. AI suggests **periodic rebalancing strategies using options**.

Trade Setup

1. AI monitors **portfolio volatility and risk exposure**, suggesting covered calls, protective puts, or iron condors when necessary.
2. AI automatically **adjusts allocations to align with market trends**.

AI Enhancement

AI detects **market shifts and portfolio drift**, ensuring **optimal risk-adjusted allocations** at all times.

Outcome Analysis

a) If the market is stable, AI **maximizes premium income via covered calls**.

b) If downside risk increases, AI **automatically shifts exposure toward hedging strategies**.

Strategy 37: AI-Based Smart Beta Options Strategy

Market Scenario

A trader wants to optimize a **factor-based investing approach** using options to enhance returns while managing risk.

Trade Setup

AI selects options trades **based on growth, value, and volatility factors**, optimizing premium collection and capital efficiency.

AI Enhancement

AI scans **fundamental and technical factors**, building an options strategy that **maximizes risk-adjusted returns**.

Outcome Analysis

a) If AI's factor models hold, **the trader outperforms standard beta investing strategies**.

b) AI suggests adjustments **when factor-based models indicate shifts in market conditions**.

Strategy 38: AI-Based Dynamic Credit Spreads for Risk Control

Market Scenario

A trader wants **consistent income** with defined risk, using AI to optimize **credit spread selection**.

Trade Setup

AI suggests selling **high-probability credit spreads**, dynamically adjusting strikes based on real-time market data.

AI Enhancement

AI monitors **implied volatility, historical win rates, and institutional flow**, selecting the most **efficient risk-reward setups**.

Outcome Analysis

a) If AI's prediction is correct, the **credit spread expires worthless**, generating full profit.

b) AI continuously scans for **early exit opportunities**, maximizing capital efficiency.

Strategy 39: AI-Powered Statistical Arbitrage in Options

Market Scenario

A trader identifies **highly correlated assets**, using AI to exploit temporary mispricings in options premiums.

Trade Setup

1. AI finds **divergences in implied volatility between correlated stocks** and suggests **pair trades**.
2. The trader **buys underpriced options on one asset and sells overpriced options on the other**.

AI Enhancement

AI scans historical correlation patterns and flags **statistical outliers**, ensuring high-probability setups.

Outcome Analysis

a) If correlation normalizes, **the trader profits from the pricing correction**.

b) AI prevents execution in **low-probability setups**, reducing risk.

Strategy 40: AI-Based Position Sizing for Optimal Returns

Market Scenario

A trader struggles with **allocating capital efficiently** across multiple options trades. AI suggests the **optimal position size based on risk-reward ratios**.

Trade Setup

1. AI assigns **capital weighting dynamically**, ensuring **balanced risk across trades**.
2. AI adjusts exposure based on **market volatility and individual trade probabilities**.

AI Enhancement

AI incorporates **portfolio risk metrics and trade confidence scores**, dynamically adjusting position sizing.

Outcome Analysis

a) If AI's sizing model is correct, the **trader maximizes gains while controlling downside risk**.

b) AI continuously recalibrates **exposure based on market changes**.

12. Advanced AI & Portfolio Optimization Strategies

Strategy 41: AI-Driven Delta Neutral Trading

Market Scenario

A trader wants to **profit from market fluctuations without taking a directional bet**. AI helps construct a **delta-neutral portfolio**, where gains and losses offset each other.

Trade Setup

1. AI suggests a **balanced mix of long and short options positions** to keep the portfolio's delta near zero.
2. Example: **Selling at-the-money puts and calls on a stock while holding stock or futures contracts to hedge price movement.**

AI Enhancement

AI continuously adjusts positions **to maintain delta neutrality**, responding to changes in volatility and market conditions.

Outcome Analysis

a) If market conditions remain stable, the **strategy profits from theta decay**.

b) AI adjusts the portfolio if delta starts **drifting in one direction**, ensuring continued neutrality.

Strategy 42: AI-Powered Implied Volatility Mean Reversion

Market Scenario

Implied volatility (IV) tends to revert to historical norms after extreme moves. AI identifies **overbought or oversold IV conditions** for profitable trades.

Trade Setup

1. AI detects an **extreme spike in implied volatility** on a stock's options chain.
2. The trader sells a **high-IV credit spread**, expecting IV to revert.

AI Enhancement

AI scans historical **implied volatility ranges**, identifying trades with the **highest statistical probability of mean reversion**.

Outcome Analysis

a) If IV declines as expected, the credit spread **profits from contracting premiums**.

b) AI monitors **changes in volatility**, suggesting early exits if mean reversion occurs faster than expected.

Strategy 43: AI-Powered Gamma Scalping for High Volatility Markets

Market Scenario

Gamma scalping involves **adjusting delta hedges to profit from volatile price swings**. AI automates gamma adjustments based on market momentum.

Trade Setup

1. AI suggests buying **at-the-money options with high gamma**, adjusting deltas dynamically.
2. The system **sells underlying shares when prices rise and buys back when they fall**, capitalizing on fluctuations.

AI Enhancement

AI tracks **volatility spikes in real time**, optimizing hedge adjustments **for maximum profit per price movement**.

Outcome Analysis

a) If volatility remains high, **gamma scalping generates consistent returns**.

b) AI prevents overtrading, ensuring **cost-effective hedge execution**.

Strategy 44: AI-Based Ratio Spread Adjustments for Low-Risk Profits

Market Scenario

A trader wants to **capture limited upside while maintaining low risk**. AI suggests the best ratio spread adjustments.

Trade Setup

AI detects **strong support/resistance levels** and suggests:

1. Buying **one call option at $100**

2. Selling **two call options at $110** for a net credit

AI Enhancement

AI adjusts the spread's **strike selection dynamically**, ensuring **optimal risk-reward ratios**.

Outcome Analysis

a) If the stock **stays within range**, the trade profits from **premium collection**.

b) If the stock moves unexpectedly, AI suggests **adjustments or rolling positions**.

Strategy 45: AI-Driven Dynamic Stop-Loss for Options Portfolios

Market Scenario

A trader wants to **protect their options portfolio** from unexpected losses. AI manages **stop-loss levels dynamically**.

Trade Setup

1. AI suggests a **tiered stop-loss system** based on market volatility.
2. The system adjusts **stop levels** in real-time to prevent premature exits.

AI Enhancement

AI continuously **monitors volatility and time decay**, tightening or loosening stop levels dynamically.

Outcome Analysis

a) If the market moves **unexpectedly**, AI stops out positions **before major losses occur**.

b) AI prevents **overly tight stops**, avoiding unnecessary position closures.

Strategy 46: AI-Based Straddle/Strangle Adjustment Strategies

Market Scenario

A trader wants to **trade high-volatility events** like earnings but avoid losing money if the stock stays flat. AI helps adjust straddle/strangle positions.

Trade Setup

1. AI suggests buying **a straddle or strangle** before a high-impact event.
2. If volatility remains low, AI rolls the trade into an **iron butterfly or iron condor**.

AI Enhancement

AI tracks **historical earnings reactions and implied volatility crush probabilities**, optimizing trade adjustments.

Outcome Analysis

a) If volatility increases, the **trade profits from directional movement**.

b) If volatility collapses, AI **adjusts to a range-bound strategy**, reducing losses.

Strategy 47: AI-Powered Automated Options Scalping Bots

Market Scenario

A trader wants **fully automated small profit trades** on high-liquidity options contracts. AI executes **scalping trades 24/7**.

Trade Setup

1. AI continuously monitors **bid-ask spreads and trading volume**.
2. The bot places **high-frequency limit orders**, capturing price inefficiencies.

AI Enhancement

AI **filters false scalping opportunities**, ensuring **only high-probability trades execute**.

Outcome Analysis

a) If spreads tighten, AI **adjusts limit orders automatically**.

b) AI prevents **overtrading**, maximizing **execution efficiency**.

Strategy 48: AI-Based Adaptive Rolling for Expiring Options

Market Scenario

A trader holds **soon-to-expire options** and wants to **extend duration while avoiding assignment risks**.

Trade Setup

1. AI detects **optimal rolling points** before expiration.
2. The trader **closes current positions and reopens similar ones in later expirations**.

AI Enhancement

AI **analyzes historical roll profitability**, selecting **the best expiration cycles and strikes**.

Outcome Analysis

a) If market conditions favor rolling, the **trader captures additional premium**.

b) AI prevents **rolling into unprofitable trades**, ensuring risk control.

Strategy 49: AI-Based Sentiment-Driven Contrarian Options Trading

Market Scenario

Social media and financial news often **drive irrational market movements**. AI detects when sentiment **reaches extreme levels** and suggests contrarian trades.

Trade Setup

1. AI detects **overly bullish sentiment** and suggests a **bearish options trade**.
2. Example: AI suggests buying **out-of-the-money puts** when excessive optimism is detected.

AI Enhancement

AI scans **Twitter, Reddit, and financial news headlines**, identifying **sentiment spikes before price reversals**.

Outcome Analysis

a) If sentiment **reverses**, the trader **profits from the correction**.

b) AI prevents **false contrarian signals**, ensuring **high-probability setups**.

Strategy 50: AI-Powered Synthetic Long/Short Stock Strategies

Market Scenario

A trader wants **stock-like exposure** with limited risk but **does not want to buy shares directly**. AI constructs synthetic stock positions using options.

Trade Setup

AI suggests a **synthetic long stock trade**:

1. Buy **$50 call option**
2. Sell **$50 put option**

AI Enhancement

AI ensures **synthetic stock positions have lower capital requirements than direct stock ownership**, adjusting **for implied volatility risks**.

Outcome Analysis

a) If the stock **rises**, the trader **profits like a shareholder** without full capital exposure.

b) AI monitors position **adjustments for optimal hedging**, reducing unnecessary risk.

13. Low-Risk Strategies (For Beginners)

Low-risk strategies are ideal for traders who are new to options and prefer consistent, predictable returns over speculative gains. These approaches prioritize income generation, capital preservation, and controlled risk exposure. AI enhances their effectiveness by pinpointing optimal market conditions for execution, boosting efficiency while minimizing potential losses.

Covered Calls

The covered call is often considered one of the safest and most practical strategies in the world of options trading. It's especially appealing to investors who already own shares and are looking for a way to generate consistent, additional income without taking on excessive risk. At its core, the strategy is straightforward: the trader holds a long position in a stock and sells a call option against those shares. The premium collected from this sale serves two purposes—it offers a degree of downside protection, and it enhances the overall return on the investment.

What makes the covered call even more powerful today is the role of artificial intelligence in refining how it's executed. AI-powered platforms now enable traders to approach this strategy with greater precision and confidence. Instead of relying solely on experience or instinct, traders can use advanced tools to identify the most promising opportunities.

For example, AI can scan the market to find stocks that exhibit a strong upward trend while maintaining low volatility—ideal conditions for a successful covered call. It can also analyze historical data to assess the likelihood of an option expiring worthless, which increases the chances of keeping the premium. Beyond that, AI models can suggest optimal strike prices based on real-time volatility and time decay dynamics, ensuring that each trade is tailored to current market conditions.

Perhaps most impressively, machine learning algorithms can detect subtle patterns, such as institutional buying activity, allowing traders to time their entries more effectively. Imagine a system that evaluates thousands of stocks and identifies the ones with high implied volatility but relatively stable prices. That combination allows the option to retain value while minimizing the risk of early assignment.

In this way, AI transforms the covered call from a simple income strategy into a disciplined, data-driven approach. It replaces guesswork with structure, intuition with insight, and offers traders a consistent edge in generating returns—without needing to constantly second-guess the market.

Cash-Secured Puts

A cash-secured put is another low-risk options strategy favored by investors who want to generate income while positioning themselves to buy high-quality stocks at a discount. The concept is simple: the trader sells a put option and holds enough cash on hand to purchase the underlying stock if assigned. This strategy is especially appealing to those who are already interested in owning a particular stock—but would prefer to buy it at a lower price, all while collecting a premium in the meantime.

If the stock stays above the strike price, the option expires worthless and the trader keeps the premium—essentially earning income without buying the stock. If the stock falls below the strike price, the trader is obligated to buy the shares, but at an effective discount once the premium is factored in. It's a win-win scenario when executed with discipline: either you collect income, or you acquire a stock you already want—just at a better price.

Artificial intelligence has added a new layer of precision to this strategy. By analyzing vast amounts of market data, AI can identify optimal opportunities that might be difficult to spot manually. For example, AI-driven platforms can scan the market for companies with strong fundamentals that are currently undervalued, reducing the risk of being assigned low-quality stocks. They also calculate strike prices with the highest statistical likelihood of expiring out of the money, helping to maximize premium income.

AI doesn't stop there—it dynamically adjusts position sizing based on real-time risk assessments and identifies periods of elevated implied volatility, which translate into richer premiums for put sellers. An advanced model might recommend selling puts only on stocks that have historically shown resilience during downturns, ensuring that any assignment leads to ownership of fundamentally sound companies.

By integrating AI into a cash-secured put strategy, traders gain the best of both worlds: consistent income and the potential to acquire quality stocks at prices that align with long-term value. It's a strategy rooted in patience and reinforced by data—ideal for investors who want to stay on the offensive, even in uncertain markets.

The Wheel Strategy

The wheel strategy is a powerful, rules-based approach that combines two of the most reliable options strategies: cash-secured puts and covered calls. It offers investors a structured way to generate consistent income while gradually building a position in a stock they're happy to own. The process begins with selling a cash-secured put on a stock the trader wouldn't mind owning. If the option is exercised and shares are assigned, the next step is to sell a covered call on those shares. Once the call expires or the shares are called away, the cycle starts again with another put—hence the name "the wheel."

What makes this strategy especially attractive for long-term investors is its dual benefit: the opportunity to collect premium income while steadily reducing the cost basis of the stock over time. It rewards patience, discipline, and a willingness to stay engaged with the same asset across multiple market cycles.

With the addition of artificial intelligence, the wheel strategy becomes even more precise and effective. AI-driven platforms can identify stocks with stable, long-term growth potential—ideal candidates for repeated option writing. They also help time the sale of puts by analyzing volatility patterns and key technical support levels, ensuring that trades are placed under favorable conditions.

Beyond timing, AI adjusts call strike prices dynamically to strike the right balance between risk and reward, especially when market momentum shifts. It also monitors portfolio exposure to prevent concentration in a single stock, an often overlooked risk when repeating trades on the same underlying asset.

For example, an AI model might suggest selling puts only during periods of low volatility to avoid sharp drawdowns, or it might tighten call strike prices when the underlying stock shows signs of losing momentum—locking in profits while maintaining the integrity of the cycle.

By incorporating AI, the wheel strategy evolves from a mechanical routine into a responsive, data-driven system. It becomes more efficient, more consistent, and ultimately more powerful—maximizing income potential while minimizing unnecessary risk.

Conclusion

Low-risk options strategies provide an excellent starting point for traders seeking consistent, low-volatility returns. Covered calls, cash-secured puts, and the wheel strategy offer predictable income streams, with AI enhancing trade selection, entry timing, and risk management.

The next section will explore moderate-risk strategies that offer greater profit potential while maintaining a balanced risk-reward profile.

14. Moderate-Risk Strategies (For Growing Capital)

Traders who have mastered the fundamentals of options trading often seek strategies that offer higher returns while maintaining controlled risk. Moderate-risk strategies strike a balance between safety and profit potential, making them ideal for traders who want to grow their capital without exposing themselves to excessive losses. These strategies incorporate a mix of income generation, directional plays, and volatility-based approaches. AI enhances these strategies by optimizing trade selection, improving entry and exit timing, and dynamically adjusting risk management parameters.

Credit Spreads (Bull Put and Bear Call)

Credit spreads are among the most popular moderate-risk strategies in options trading. They involve selling one option and buying another at a different strike price—limiting potential loss while collecting premium income. The net credit received represents the maximum profit if the trade plays out favorably.

A **bull put spread** is used when expecting the stock to stay flat or rise modestly: the trader sells a higher-strike put and buys a lower-strike put, defining both risk and reward. Conversely, a **bear call spread** profits when the stock remains below a certain level: the trader sells a lower-strike call and buys a higher-strike call.

AI enhances these strategies by identifying high-probability setups based on trends, volatility, and historical behavior. It spots overstated implied volatility—ideal for selling premium—and selects strike prices that maximize return while keeping risk in check.

Iron Condors

The iron condor is a market-neutral strategy designed to profit from low volatility. It combines a bull put spread and a bear call spread on the same asset, creating a defined profit range. As long as the asset stays within this range, the trader keeps the premium. Risk is capped—limited to the distance between strikes minus the credit received.

This setup is ideal when the market is moving sideways. AI takes the strategy further by analyzing volatility cycles, spotting stable trading ranges, and flagging assets with low implied volatility—perfect conditions for iron condors.

AI also adapts positions in real time. If price action breaks out, it can suggest rolling spreads or adjusting strikes to manage risk. It even helps avoid poor timing by selecting expiration dates that steer clear of earnings or major economic events.

Diagonal Spreads

A diagonal spread blends elements of a calendar and vertical spread, allowing traders to profit from both time decay and directional movement. It involves buying a long-term option while selling a shorter-term option at a different strike price—capturing premium while retaining exposure to longer-term trends.

This strategy works best when gradual price movement is expected, rather than sharp volatility. AI enhances diagonal spreads by analyzing time decay patterns and identifying stocks with consistent behavior across expirations.

AI-powered platforms can fine-tune strike and expiration selection based on volatility forecasts, and dynamically adjust the position as conditions change—rolling, hedging, or rebalancing to keep the trade aligned with the market.

Conclusion

Moderate-risk strategies offer a smart way to grow capital while keeping risk well-defined. Techniques like credit spreads, iron condors, and diagonal spreads let traders capitalize on market conditions with clear parameters for profit and loss. AI takes these strategies further—enhancing trade selection, fine-tuning risk management, and adapting positions in real time as markets evolve.

Up next: high-risk, high-reward strategies for traders ready to embrace greater volatility in pursuit of outsized returns.

15. High-Risk, High-Reward Strategies (For Aggressive Traders)

Some traders seek high returns and are willing to take on greater risk in pursuit of larger rewards. High-risk options strategies provide significant profit potential, but they also expose traders to substantial losses if the market moves against them. These strategies require a deep understanding of options pricing, market behavior, and risk management. AI can help mitigate some of the risks by identifying optimal conditions for execution, improving position sizing, and adjusting strategies based on real-time data.

Naked Options (Selling Puts and Calls)

Selling naked options—also known as uncovered options—is among the riskiest strategies in options trading. Unlike covered or cash-secured positions, it involves selling options without holding the underlying asset or sufficient collateral, exposing the trader to potentially unlimited losses.

Naked puts are sold without cash reserves to buy the stock if assigned. While profitable if the stock stays above the strike, a sharp drop can force the trader to buy at a loss. **Naked calls** are even riskier: if the stock price surges, the trader must buy shares at market value to cover the position, leading to substantial, theoretically unlimited losses.

AI can help mitigate some of this risk. By analyzing historical volatility and forecasting price stability, AI systems reduce the likelihood of trading in highly volatile conditions. Real-time monitoring and automated hedging tools can also intervene if the market moves unexpectedly, limiting downside before losses spiral out of control.

Butterfly Spreads

The butterfly spread is a defined-risk strategy built to profit from low volatility and minimal price movement. It combines long and short options at three strike prices, aiming for maximum profit if the stock lands on the middle strike at expiration.

A **call butterfly** involves buying one lower-strike call, selling two at-the-money calls, and buying one higher-strike call. The **put butterfly** follows the same structure with puts.

While the potential reward is high relative to risk, execution must be precise, and the strategy works best in calm markets. AI enhances butterfly spreads by identifying assets with historically low volatility and selecting strike prices with the highest probability of success. If conditions shift, AI tools can dynamically adjust the position to protect or improve outcomes.

Strangles and Straddles

Straddles and strangles are volatility-based strategies designed to profit from sharp price moves in either direction. Both involve buying a call and a put simultaneously, allowing traders to benefit regardless of whether the market moves up or down.

A **long straddle** uses the same strike and expiration for both options—ideal when a big move is expected, but the direction is uncertain. A **long strangle** lowers entry cost by using different strikes: a higher one for the call, a lower one for the put. This setup requires a larger price move to be profitable but offers more flexibility.

AI enhances these strategies by identifying high-volatility setups, such as pre-earnings or news-driven events. It analyzes sentiment, historical reactions, and order flow to pinpoint assets primed for a breakout. AI can also adjust trades mid-course—suggesting rolls or extensions if the anticipated move hasn't materialized yet.

Conclusion

High-risk, high-reward strategies offer the potential for substantial gains—but they demand precision, discipline, and robust risk management. Tactics like naked options, butterfly spreads, and volatility plays such as straddles and strangles require sharp timing and a clear read on market behavior.

AI strengthens these approaches by pinpointing ideal setups, managing risk dynamically, and adapting positions in real time. Traders willing to embrace the volatility must also respect the risk—and with AI-driven tools, they can do so with greater confidence and control.

CHAPTER 7: AVOIDING COSTLY TRADING MISTAKES WITH AI

Picture this: you're making solid trades, watching profits roll in—until one unexpected move wipes out your gains. That's why managing risk is such a critical component of successful options trading.

While many traders focus on maximizing profits, neglecting safeguards can lead to devastating losses. Traditionally, this has meant setting stop-losses, diversifying portfolios, and maintaining disciplined position sizing.

Today, with the rise of artificial intelligence, traders can harness machine learning to evaluate potential threats dynamically and make informed decisions that improve resilience to market fluctuations.

Intelligent automation has revolutionized how investors assess downside exposure, implement hedging strategies, and allocate capital more effectively. By processing vast datasets, these systems can uncover subtle patterns in market behavior, assign probability-based risk scores, and adapt strategies in real time.

The first step in leveraging smart technology for capital protection is understanding how these tools function and how major institutions apply them to limit losses while optimizing gains.

1. Using AI for Risk Assessment

One of the biggest advantages artificial intelligence offers in trading is its ability to calculate and assign tailored risk scores to individual trades and entire portfolios. Unlike traditional methods, which rely on static indicators like volatility or drawdown thresholds, AI evaluates a much broader range of real-time factors—including market sentiment, historical price behavior, macroeconomic trends, and even geopolitical developments.

This advanced evaluation is particularly valuable in options trading, where leverage can amplify both profits and losses. A poorly calculated move can lead to substantial damage if exposure isn't controlled appropriately. By continuously monitoring market dynamics, AI systems adjust protective parameters on the fly, helping traders stay ahead of potential downturns.

AI-Generated Risk Scores

AI-generated risk scores provide a quantitative snapshot of a trade's potential downside. These metrics are derived from factors such as historical and implied volatility, liquidity, and price correlations. By assigning a numerical value to each setup, machine learning tools help traders evaluate whether the expected return justifies the potential exposure.

For instance, an algorithm might assess an options trade using market history, news sentiment, and flow data—concluding there's a high likelihood of significant price movement. If the system assigns a score of 85 out of 100, it indicates elevated risk, suggesting the need for additional hedging or a smaller position size. Here's how traders can make the most of these risk scores:

1. Focus on lower-risk opportunities when markets are uncertain when market conditions are uncertain

2. Adjust position sizing based on calculated risk levels.

3. Avoid taking high-risk trades without proper hedging mechanisms.

Some AI-powered trading platforms embed these evaluations directly into their execution engines, automatically blocking trades that would breach preset exposure limits. This prevents traders from unintentionally taking on excessive downside.

What makes these dynamic assessments particularly valuable is their adaptability—they evolve in real time with shifting market landscapes. Unlike static models that rely solely on past data, intelligent systems continuously refine their analysis as fresh inputs arrive. In the event of a spike in volatility caused by unexpected news or economic developments, the algorithm can instantly adjust its evaluation and suggest safer alternative strategies.

How Hedge Funds Use AI to Minimize Risk

Hedge funds and institutional investors have leveraged artificial intelligence for risk mitigation long before it became accessible to the average trader. While retail participants often rely on basic tools like stop-losses or diversification, professional firms embed AI directly into their trading systems to reduce exposure and enhance returns.

One of their core strategies involves predictive modeling. By processing massive datasets, these intelligent systems can detect early warning signs of heightened market instability. For example, an AI model might identify:

⇒ A rise in short interest on a particular stock, indicating potential bearish sentiment.

⇒ A spike in implied volatility ahead of an earnings announcement, suggesting heightened uncertainty.

⇒ A shift in institutional order flow, where large investors are reducing positions in a specific sector.

By detecting early warning signals, professional traders can rebalance their portfolios before a downturn unfolds, effectively reducing their exposure in advance.

Another way institutional investors leverage artificial intelligence is through adaptive hedging techniques. While traditional methods typically involve buying protective puts or spreading risk across asset classes, AI enhances these approaches by:

⇒ Dynamically adjusting hedge ratios based on real-time market conditions.

⇒ Identifying the most cost-effective hedging instruments based on current options pricing.

⇒ Rebalancing portfolios to maintain an optimal risk-reward balance as market conditions evolve.

For example, if a system detects increased downside exposure for a specific stock, it may recommend rolling a covered call into a protective put spread—offering added protection without greatly limiting upside potential.

In addition, institutional investors employ AI-powered stress testing tools to simulate a wide range of market scenarios and assess their potential impact on portfolio performance. These simulations help uncover vulnerabilities in the overall strategy, allowing for proactive adjustments before losses materialize.

Advanced risk monitoring is equally vital for high-frequency trading firms, where decisions are made in milliseconds. Here, AI is essential for spotting anomalies in order flow, market depth, and price action—enabling rapid exits before small errors escalate into major losses.

As artificial intelligence continues to evolve, managing risk is expected to become more automated and accurate. Many of the advanced tools once reserved for hedge funds are now accessible to individual investors. By incorporating these technologies into their strategies, traders can better shield themselves from unexpected market swings and boost long-term performance.

The next section explores how AI enhances position sizing and portfolio allocation—helping traders deploy capital more efficiently while maintaining a well-balanced exposure.

2. AI-Powered Position Sizing

Proper position sizing plays a vital role in managing risk when trading options. Even a well-researched setup can lead to losses if funds are allocated inefficiently. A common mistake among traders is either overleveraging—committing too much to a single trade—or underinvesting, which can result in missed opportunities.

Traditional methods often rely on fixed percentage rules or standard risk/reward ratios, but these static models struggle to adapt to market fluctuations.

Modern AI-based systems have transformed this process by introducing dynamic allocation strategies. These tools assess market volatility, historical win rates, asset correlations, and real-time risk to help traders deploy the right amount of capital to each position—maximizing performance while minimizing unnecessary exposure.

Smart Allocation with Machine Learning

Machine learning models evaluate both historical and real-time trading data to determine the ideal position size for each setup. Unlike traditional fixed-percentage rules, these systems adapt dynamically, factoring in market conditions, portfolio exposure, and past performance.

One of the key innovations is volatility-adjusted allocation. Since markets evolve constantly, the level of risk associated with a trade can shift from one day to the next. Intelligent models account for:

1. **Historical asset volatility**: If an asset has shown frequent price swings, the system may reduce allocation to limit potential losses.
2. **Current implied volatility**: A spike in implied volatility, often linked to upcoming events like earnings, signals elevated uncertainty—prompting a more cautious allocation.
3. **Correlation with active positions**: When a new trade closely mirrors existing ones, the system may reduce size to avoid overexposure in a single market direction.

For instance, if a sudden rise in implied volatility is detected ahead of a company's earnings release, the model might scale down the size of an options position to reflect the increased uncertainty. Conversely, in a more stable environment, it may raise allocation to capitalize on reduced risk.

These smart allocation techniques also incorporate historical strategy performance. If a trader's approach has delivered strong results in similar contexts, the system may assign greater weight to the trade. On the other hand, a lower historical success rate could lead to a reduced size—or suggest skipping the opportunity entirely.

AI-Based Portfolio Balancing Techniques

Maintaining long-term stability and consistent returns requires more than just picking the right trades—it demands thoughtful capital distribution across a range of assets, sectors, and strategies.

While many traders focus narrowly on individual positions, a properly structured portfolio helps reduce overall exposure and cushions against volatility.

Intelligent rebalancing systems go a step further than traditional diversification, continuously adjusting allocations based on evolving market conditions. Instead of following a static model, these tools shift weightings in real time by analyzing performance trends, risk indicators, and predictive signals.

How AI Optimizes Portfolio Balance

1. **Real-Time Correlation Analysis**

AI continuously monitors how assets within a portfolio relate to one another. When multiple trades share similar risk exposures, the system may adjust allocations to reduce overlap. For instance, if a trader holds several bullish options in tech, it might recommend trimming those positions and reallocating capital to other areas like consumer goods or energy to improve diversification.

2. **Risk-Weighted Allocation Adjustments**

AI assesses the risk-reward ratio of each open trade and automatically redistributes capital based on risk exposure.

a) If a certain trade is becoming riskier (due to a rise in implied volatility or negative sentiment analysis), AI may reduce its weighting in the portfolio.

b) If a safer trade is identified (low volatility, high probability of profit), AI may increase allocation to balance risk.

3. Position Scaling Based on Market Conditions

These systems track macroeconomic indicators, news sentiment, and institutional flows to anticipate market movements. When a potential downturn is identified, they may scale back exposure to riskier trades and reallocate funds toward more defensive assets.

4. Dynamic Rebalancing Based on Strategy Performance

AI assesses the performance of various trading approaches, identifying which ones are gaining traction and which are falling behind. Rather than following a fixed allocation plan, it reallocates capital toward strategies with stronger success potential.

a) If AI identifies that credit spreads are yielding better returns than iron condors in a given market cycle, it may recommend increasing exposure to credit spreads.

b) If volatility-based strategies are underperforming due to a period of low market volatility, AI may suggest pivoting to trend-following strategies.

5. Capital Efficiency Through AI-Driven Leverage

Certain intelligent trading systems refine capital allocation by assessing when leverage is appropriate and when a cautious stance is preferable. In low-risk environments, they may suggest using leverage to enhance returns, while in volatile periods, they scale back and favor more defensive holdings.

Practical Example of AI-Based Position Sizing in Action

Imagine a trader has a $100,000 portfolio and is considering placing multiple options trades. Without AI, they might use a fixed 5% allocation per trade, meaning each position would receive a $5,000 investment, regardless of market conditions.

With AI, position sizing is dynamically adjusted based on multiple risk factors. Suppose AI determines:

a) Trade A has a high probability of success based on historical patterns and low volatility → AI allocates $7,000 instead of $5,000 to maximize profit potential.

b) Trade B carries higher risk due to upcoming earnings and high implied volatility → AI reduces the allocation to $3,000 instead of $5,000.

c) Trade C is strongly correlated with Trade A, increasing portfolio concentration risk → AI limits exposure and suggests an alternative trade.

By applying AI-driven position sizing, the trader optimizes capital allocation, reduces unnecessary risk, and increases the probability of long-term success.

Conclusion

Smart position sizing and dynamic portfolio balancing mark a major step forward in risk control. Instead of relying on fixed rules, these systems adjust trade sizes and capital distribution in real time based on shifting market conditions, probability of success, and overall exposure.

By integrating AI into their position sizing strategy, traders gain a powerful edge in capital management. AI enables them to **optimize efficiency** by allocating funds to high-probability trades, **minimize correlation risk** through diversified exposure, and **adjust position sizes dynamically** in response to volatility and shifting market trends. Most importantly, AI helps **maximize long-term profitability** by continuously reallocating capital toward the most effective and proven strategies.

The next section will explore how AI helps traders maintain emotional discipline, preventing impulsive decisions and automating execution to reduce human error.

3. Emotional Discipline with AI

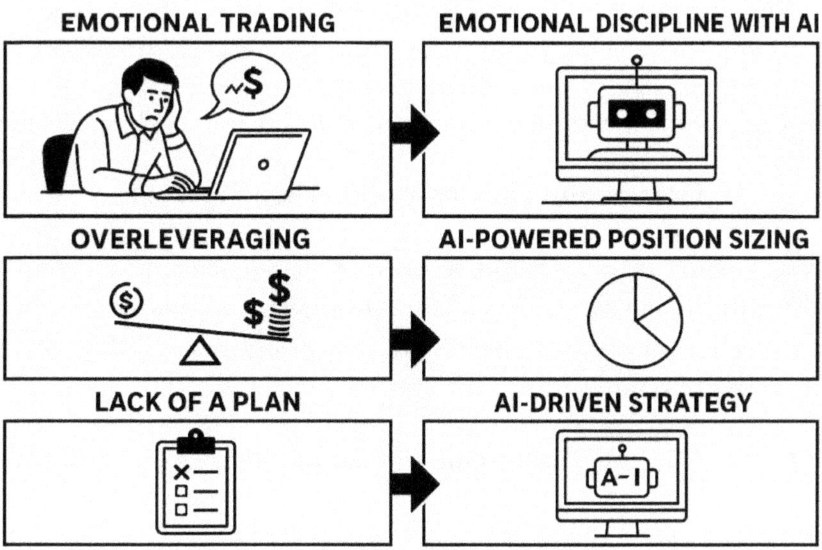

One of the biggest challenges in trading is managing emotions. Feelings like fear, greed, hesitation, and overconfidence can cloud judgment, often leading to poor decisions that undermine profits and increase risk. Even seasoned traders can struggle with emotional control—especially during turbulent markets.

Modern algorithms now offer a powerful tool for promoting discipline. By filtering out emotional bias, intelligent systems help traders steer clear of panic selling, overtrading, and impulsive moves. With constant market analysis, they issue alerts when emotional interference is detected and can even automate execution to keep strategies on track.

AI-Generated Alerts for Emotional Trading

AI excels at spotting emotional trading patterns by examining a trader's past behavior, current market context, and decision-making habits. Many fall into common psychological traps without realizing it—like chasing losses or doubling down out of overconfidence. Smart alerts identify these patterns in real time, helping traders respond with clarity instead of emotion.

Some of the most common emotional trading patterns AI detects include:

A. Overtrading after losses (Revenge Trading)

When a trader takes consecutive losses, they may attempt to immediately recover by placing excessive trades. AI recognizes this pattern and issues an alert, encouraging the trader to step back and reassess before making impulsive decisions.

B. Chasing Trades Due to Fear of Missing Out (FOMO)

Many traders enter trades at suboptimal prices because they see the market moving and fear missing out on a big move. AI scans for FOMO-driven entries and warns traders when a trade does not meet pre-established risk-reward criteria.

C. Ignoring Stop-Losses Due to Hope

One of the most dangerous emotional mistakes traders make is refusing to exit a losing trade, hoping that the market will reverse. AI monitors stop-loss adherence and alerts traders if they hesitate to close a position that has already exceeded a predefined risk threshold.

D. Greed-Based Position Sizing

Some traders increase position sizes dramatically after a winning streak, believing they are on a "hot streak." AI detects deviation from normal position sizing behavior and alerts traders if they are risking too much capital on a single trade.

E. Panic Selling in Volatile Markets

When markets experience sharp declines, traders often make impulsive decisions, liquidating positions out of fear rather than strategic analysis. AI evaluates market conditions and historical price behavior to determine whether a sell-off is an opportunity for reentry or if exiting is truly the best decision.

By integrating AI-generated alerts into their trading routines, traders gain an objective, data-driven warning system that helps prevent costly emotional mistakes. These alerts function as a psychological buffer, allowing traders to re-evaluate their decisions before acting impulsively.

Automated Trade Execution to Avoid Panic Selling

Even with smart alerts in place, many traders still find it difficult to stay emotionally disciplined. In fast-moving markets, instincts often override planning, leading to impulsive decisions that derail solid strategies. To counter this, automation takes over—executing trades based on logic rather than emotion.

Rule-based execution systems rely on predefined criteria and real-time data, giving traders the ability to:

A. Automatically execute stop-losses and take-profits without hesitation

AI enforces discipline by ensuring that traders do not manually override stop-loss or take-profit levels due to emotional bias.

B. Implement AI-powered trailing stops to capture profits

Many traders exit winning trades too soon out of fear that profits will evaporate. AI dynamically adjusts trailing stops based on volatility, securing profits while still allowing for upside potential.

C. Scale out of positions systematically

Instead of exiting an entire position at once, AI can gradually reduce exposure based on pre-set rules. This method helps traders capture maximum gains while managing risk.

D. Lock in profits when extreme market conditions are detected

AI analyzes news sentiment, institutional order flow, and macroeconomic indicators to determine when high-impact market events may justify closing a position early.

E. **Prevent impulsive trading outside of predefined strategy parameters**

AI-driven trading systems ensure that traders only take trades that align with their predefined strategies, reducing the temptation to place random trades based on emotion.

A clear example of intelligent execution is automated rebalancing. When emotional bias leads to overexposure in a single sector, the system can adjust positions automatically to restore balance. Likewise, it can block trades in overhyped stocks by requiring that certain valuation thresholds be met before proceeding.

AI as an Emotional Buffer for Traders

One of the most underrated benefits of AI in risk management is its ability to act as an emotional buffer, allowing traders to maintain a systematic, rules-based approach to the markets. Rather than making decisions based on fear, greed, or uncertainty, traders rely on AI-driven insights and execution mechanisms to stay consistent.

By integrating AI-powered emotional discipline tools, traders can significantly improve psychological control and execution quality. These tools help **reduce panic selling** and impulsive entries, **enhance consistency** by reinforcing adherence to AI-generated signals, and **prevent destructive behaviors** like revenge trading or overleveraging. Most importantly, they keep traders anchored to **data-driven decisions**, allowing logic—not emotion—to guide their actions in volatile markets.

AI does not eliminate human judgment, but it enhances discipline by providing real-time feedback, enforcing risk limits, and ensuring that trades align with logical strategy parameters.

Conclusion

Emotional trading remains one of the biggest obstacles to long-term success in options trading. AI-driven risk management tools provide traders with alerts, automated execution, and systematic trade enforcement to ensure that decision-making remains rational and disciplined.

By leveraging AI, traders can develop a structured, emotion-free approach that protects them from psychological pitfalls and maximizes long-term profitability.

PART 3:

MASTERING THE MARKET WITH AI & LONG-TERM SUCCESS

CHAPTER 8: BUILDING AN AI-DRIVEN TRADING PLAN

A successful trader does not rely on random market movements or gut instincts. Instead, they operate with a structured plan that outlines clear objectives, risk parameters, and execution strategies. An AI-driven trading plan takes this a step further by integrating machine learning models, automated decision-making, and real-time data analysis to optimize trading outcomes.

Setting clear goals is the foundation of any trading plan. Without well-defined objectives, traders may fall into inconsistent behavior, leading to unnecessary risk and emotional decision-making. AI enhances goal setting by providing data-driven insights into risk tolerance, expected returns, and trade performance tracking.

1. Setting Clear Goals

A well-structured trading plan should begin with specific and measurable goals. Traders need to define their risk tolerance, profit expectations, and preferred trading style. These goals serve as a guideline for AI-driven systems, allowing algorithms to align trading strategies with an individual's financial objectives.

Risk tolerance is a key factor in building a trading plan. Every trader has a different level of comfort when it comes to potential losses. Some are willing to accept higher volatility for the chance of larger returns, while others prioritize capital preservation. AI systems assess historical trading behavior, market trends, and portfolio performance to recommend risk settings that match individual preferences.

Defining profit targets is equally important. Setting realistic expectations ensures that traders do not fall into the trap of overtrading or holding positions too long out of greed. AI analyzes historical trade performance, asset volatility, and macroeconomic trends to suggest optimal profit targets. These targets are not static but adjust dynamically based on market conditions.

For example, if AI detects a period of heightened market uncertainty, it may recommend lower profit targets to secure gains before potential reversals. In contrast, during strong trending markets, AI may suggest extending profit-taking points to capture larger price movements.

AI also helps traders set realistic win-rate expectations based on historical backtesting. Many traders overestimate their success rate, leading to poor risk-reward calculations. By evaluating past trades and market conditions, AI provides a probability-based approach to setting realistic expectations, helping traders refine their strategies.

AI-Based Journaling and Trade Tracking

One of the greatest challenges traders face is learning effectively from their own performance. Without a structured system to track trades, many fall into patterns of repeated mistakes and missed opportunities for growth. AI-driven journaling and trade tracking tools solve this by automatically recording and analyzing every trade in real time.

These intelligent systems capture key data points—entry and exit levels, market conditions, risk-reward ratios, and even emotional context, such as whether a decision followed a strategy or was emotionally driven. Rather than relying on manual note-taking, AI organizes trades into performance categories, highlighting patterns that distinguish winning trades from losing ones.

Traders receive actionable insights, such as:

- ⇒ Which trade types have the highest success rate
- ⇒ How emotions are impacting execution
- ⇒ Whether stop-losses and take-profits are optimally placed

Beyond metrics, AI tools also flag behavioral tendencies. If a trader consistently exits too early or overrides stop-losses, the system can issue tailored alerts and suggest adjustments—helping to break unproductive habits and refine discipline.

In short, AI-powered journaling transforms trade tracking from a chore into a powerful feedback loop—turning every trade, win or lose, into a learning opportunity.

For example, if a trader tends to close winning trades before reaching full profit potential, AI may suggest adjusting trailing stop parameters or increasing profit targets based on historical data.

Another advantage of AI-powered trade tracking is real-time performance benchmarking. AI compares a trader's performance to market conditions, identifying whether a given strategy is performing better or worse than expected. If AI detects a prolonged period of underperformance, it can suggest modifications to improve execution.

Automated journaling also plays a crucial role in backtesting, which will be covered in the next section. By maintaining a detailed record of past trades, AI enhances the ability to refine strategies before implementing them in live markets.

Setting clear goals and tracking progress with AI ensures that traders maintain consistency and discipline, reducing the likelihood of impulsive decision-making. The integration of AI into goal setting and trade journaling provides an objective, data-driven approach to improving long-term trading performance.

2. Developing a Backtesting Strategy

No trading strategy is complete without rigorous testing. Backtesting allows traders to evaluate their strategies using historical market data before committing real capital. A well-structured backtesting process helps traders identify weaknesses, optimize parameters, and increase confidence in their approach.

Traditional backtesting involves manually reviewing historical price charts and applying a strategy to past market movements. While this method can offer insights, it is time-consuming and prone to human bias. AI-driven backtesting, on the other hand, automates the process, performing thousands of simulations in minutes while identifying patterns that human traders might overlook.

How to Simulate Trades Before Risking Real Money

Backtesting is essential for determining whether a trading strategy has a statistical edge. If a strategy does not perform well in simulated market conditions, it is unlikely to succeed in live trading. AI significantly improves the backtesting process by incorporating large datasets, reducing human error, and optimizing trade execution models.

A well-structured AI-powered backtesting framework consists of several steps:

a. Defining the Strategy Parameters

Before running a backtest, traders must clearly define the rules of their strategy. These include:

1. Entry and exit conditions
2. Position sizing rules
3. Risk management parameters (stop-loss, take-profit levels)
4. Market conditions (volatility filters, trend direction, liquidity constraints)

AI refines these parameters by analyzing past market conditions and recommending adjustments based on profitability metrics. Instead of relying on fixed stop-loss values or rigid profit targets, AI dynamically suggests adaptive thresholds that improve over time.

b. Selecting Historical Data for Testing

The quality of historical data used in backtesting is critical to strategy reliability. AI-driven platforms enhance this process by analyzing a wide range of scenarios—including bull, bear, and sideways markets—while accounting for asset-specific behaviors and macroeconomic factors like interest rate shifts, earnings releases, and major news events.

By testing strategies across diverse conditions, AI prevents over-optimization for a single market environment, ensuring more robust and adaptable performance in live trading.

c. Running the Backtest and Collecting Performance Metrics

AI-driven backtesting engines simulate trades at high speed, replicating how a strategy would have performed under real market conditions. These simulations reveal critical performance metrics such as win and loss rates, risk-adjusted returns, maximum drawdown, and Sharpe ratio—offering a clear picture of both profitability and risk efficiency.

What sets AI apart is its ability to continuously refine strategy parameters. If it detects, for instance, that a specific stop-loss level causes excessive drawdowns, it will recommend adjustments to optimize risk management and improve overall performance.

d. Detecting Overfitting and Optimizing the Strategy

One of the key pitfalls in backtesting is overfitting—when a strategy is overly tailored to historical data but fails in live markets. AI reduces this risk through **walk-forward testing** and **out-of-sample validation**.

Walk-forward testing applies the strategy to unseen data, confirming its consistency across varying market conditions. Out-of-sample validation splits historical data into training and testing sets to ensure the strategy isn't just reacting to the past, but demonstrates real predictive power in future scenarios.

By automating these processes, AI-driven backtesting provides a data-driven, unbiased evaluation of a trading strategy's effectiveness, improving the likelihood of success in live markets.

Using AI for Market Pattern Recognition

One of AI's greatest strengths in trading is its ability to detect complex market patterns that may not be visible to human traders. Traditional technical analysis relies on static chart patterns such as head and shoulders, double tops, and triangles. AI, however, goes beyond static recognition by identifying dynamic, evolving market structures and detecting patterns that may indicate future price movements.

AI-powered pattern recognition works by analyzing vast amounts of historical data to uncover hidden relationships between price, volume, and market sentiment. Unlike traditional methods that require traders to manually scan charts, AI can process millions of price points in seconds, identifying recurring patterns with high predictive accuracy.

1. Identifying Repetitive Price Action Sequences

One of the key pitfalls in backtesting is overfitting—when a strategy is overly tailored to historical data but fails in live markets. AI reduces this risk through **walk-forward testing** and **out-of-sample validation**.

Walk-forward testing applies the strategy to unseen data, confirming its consistency across varying market conditions. Out-of-sample validation splits historical data into training and testing sets to ensure the strategy isn't just reacting to the past, but demonstrates real predictive power in future scenarios.

2. Analyzing Sentiment-Driven Market Movements

AI integrates news sentiment, earnings reports, and social media discussions into pattern recognition models. For example, if AI detects a similar news-driven price reaction in multiple historical instances, it may predict a high-probability trade setup based on sentiment shifts.

3. Optimizing Entry and Exit Timing Based on Pattern Strength

When AI detects a potential market pattern, it goes beyond recognition—it quantifies opportunity. It calculates **optimal entry points** based on past behavior, defines **risk-adjusted stop-loss and take-profit levels**, and assesses the **likelihood of continuation versus reversal**.

Crucially, AI doesn't treat all patterns equally. Each setup is assigned a **confidence score** based on historical accuracy, helping traders focus on high-probability opportunities with greater precision.

4. Automating Pattern-Based Trade Execution

AI-driven trading bots can autonomously recognize chart patterns and execute trades based on predefined rules—eliminating subjective bias and ensuring timely, disciplined execution. For instance, if the system identifies a descending triangle with a 75% historical probability of breaking downward, it can instantly deploy a bearish options strategy, such as a bear put spread or short call.

When integrated into backtesting, AI-powered pattern recognition provides several key advantages:

⇒ **Objective, data-driven confirmation** before trade execution
⇒ **Filtering of false signals** and avoidance of overfitted setups
⇒ **Improved timing** through probability-based pattern analysis

This fusion of automation and analytics turns pattern recognition into a precise, performance-driven tool—helping traders act with clarity and confidence.

Conclusion

A solid backtesting strategy is crucial for validating and refining trading approaches before risking real capital. AI elevates this process by running simulations across vast datasets, using adaptive validation to prevent overfitting, and uncovering hidden market patterns with predictive value.

With AI-driven pattern recognition, traders gain a powerful analytical edge—designing higher-probability strategies that reflect historical market behavior. The result is a more disciplined, data-driven decision-making process that removes guesswork and builds confidence before entering live trades.

CHAPTER 9: AUTOMATING YOUR TRADING ROUTINE

As financial markets become more data-driven, traders who embrace automation and AI-powered execution gain a significant edge. AI not only enhances trade timing and risk management, but it also filters market noise, detects institutional activity, and reacts faster than human traders.

This chapter explores AI-powered trade execution and market sentiment analysis, showing how automation can help traders execute smarter, faster, and more efficient trades.

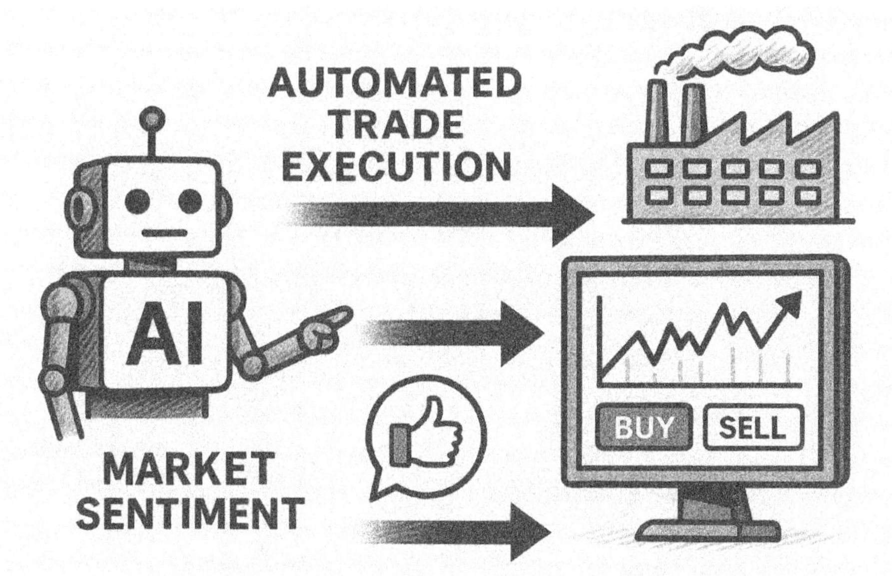

1. AI-Powered Trade Execution

As financial markets become increasingly complex, traders are turning to AI-powered execution systems to gain an edge. Traditional manual trading is often slow, emotion-driven, and prone to inefficiencies, while AI-powered automation ensures faster execution, better decision-making, and optimized risk management.

AI-driven trade execution allows traders to eliminate human error, automate repetitive tasks, and execute trades based on real-time market conditions. Whether you're a beginner exploring semi-automated trading or an experienced trader looking for fully autonomous AI-driven execution, understanding how these systems work is crucial.

This section will break down how auto-trading bots function, their advantages, and the best platforms for integrating AI into your trading routine.

Auto-Trading Bots and How to Use Them

The use of auto-trading bots has skyrocketed in recent years as AI technology continues to evolve. These bots scan markets, detect high-probability trade setups, and execute orders automatically, removing human bias and emotional decision-making from trading.

Unlike traditional trading, where traders manually analyze charts and place trades, AI-driven bots allow for systematic, rule-based execution, ensuring better efficiency, precision, and consistency. However, understanding how to use them effectively is key to leveraging their full potential.

The Rise of Automated Trading

Automated trading, once reserved for institutional investors and hedge funds, is now accessible to retail traders through AI-powered trading platforms. AI has made it possible for individual traders to execute algorithmic strategies, manage risk in real-time, and optimize trades without needing constant market monitoring.

While some traders may hesitate to give up manual control, the reality is that AI can analyze thousands of data points in milliseconds, making trade decisions far more efficient and data-driven than human traders can achieve. Automated trading also eliminates emotional bias, one of the biggest obstacles to profitable trading.

Many traders struggle with exiting winning trades too early or holding onto losing trades too long, but AI-driven execution ensures logical, disciplined, and pre-defined trade execution. Understanding how AI trading bots work is essential for integrating them into a successful trading routine.

How Auto-Trading Bots Work

An auto-trading bot operates by following a predefined algorithm that adjusts trades dynamically based on current market conditions. It begins by scanning real-time data streams to identify potential trade opportunities. Once a promising setup is detected, the bot processes the signal using its trading logic—whether it's a moving average crossover, a shift in implied volatility, or a sentiment forecast generated by AI. If all predefined criteria are met, it executes the trade automatically, without human intervention.

From there, the bot manages risk in real time, adjusting stop-loss levels, taking profits, or deploying hedging strategies as needed. Over time, it analyzes past trades and continuously optimizes its performance, evolving with each market cycle to improve execution and decision-making.

Real-World Example: AI-Driven Options Trading Bot

Imagine an AI-powered options trading bot engineered specifically to sell covered calls on high-probability stocks. It begins by scanning the market for equities with historically low volatility and consistent upward trends. Using machine learning models trained on past expiration data, it identifies the optimal strike prices and timing for execution—entering the trade at precisely the right moment to capture maximum premium.

If market conditions shift, the bot can automatically roll the position forward, maintaining cash flow while minimizing the risk of assignment. With each cycle, it learns from previous trades, refining its strategy and enhancing its ability to pinpoint the most profitable opportunities.

Best Platforms for Automated Options Trading

Several platforms now offer powerful AI-driven tools for automating options trading, each catering to different styles and experience levels.

Trade Ideas is known for its real-time stock and options scanning capabilities, powered by AI that identifies high-probability setups. It's particularly suited for short-term momentum traders and options scalpers who rely on speed and precision.

Tickeron delivers AI-generated trade signals with detailed win-rate analytics, helping traders identify optimal strike prices and expiration dates. It's a great match for swing traders and those who use multi-leg options strategies like spreads.

Option Alpha offers a fully automated trading framework where users create rule-based bots to execute strategies such as credit spreads, iron condors, and straddles. It's ideal for those seeking hands-off execution based on pre-defined conditions.

QuantConnect stands out for traders looking to develop and rigorously backtest custom AI algorithms. It supports institutional-grade testing across thousands of historical data points, making it perfect for advanced traders building proprietary systems.

The right platform depends on your goals—whether you're after simplicity, flexibility, speed, or full customization. AI automation in options trading is now more accessible than ever; the key is aligning the tools with your specific strategy and risk profile.

2. Using AI for Market News & Sentiment Analysis

Financial markets are heavily influenced by news, economic events, and investor sentiment. In today's fast-paced trading environment, where millions of data points are generated daily, manually analyzing market sentiment is nearly impossible.

This is where AI-powered sentiment analysis comes into play. AI scans and interprets news reports, social media trends, institutional reports, and financial statements in real-time, helping traders detect market shifts before they happen.

Understanding how AI analyzes, filters, and predicts market sentiment gives traders an edge, allowing them to act on high-confidence signals rather than reacting emotionally.

How AI Predicts Market Shifts Before They Happen

One of the most powerful applications of AI in trading is predictive sentiment analysis. AI can identify early signs of bullish or bearish sentiment, giving traders an opportunity to enter or exit trades before the rest of the market reacts.

Traditional traders rely on technical indicators, news headlines, and economic reports, but AI can process millions of data points simultaneously, uncovering hidden patterns and correlations that would take humans days or weeks to analyze.

By continuously monitoring market conditions, AI-powered systems can:

a) **Detect unusual trading activity** that signals large institutional moves.

b) **Identify sentiment shifts in news coverage** before they affect stock prices.

c) **Analyze social media and financial reports** for high-impact trends.

Understanding how AI processes this information allows traders to execute better-timed trades and avoid emotional decision-making.

The Role of Market Sentiment in Trading

Market sentiment—shaped by news headlines, social media chatter, and investor emotions—has a profound influence on price movements. While technical indicators are useful for identifying historical trends, they often miss the subtle, real-time shifts in sentiment that trigger sudden volatility.

Take earnings season, for example. A company might post strong quarterly results, yet issue cautious forward guidance. While traditional metrics may still point upward, AI models can detect negative sentiment embedded in management's language or online investor reactions, flagging a potential reversal before it plays out on the charts.

Similarly, a baseless rumor spreading across social platforms can provoke panic selling. Human traders might react emotionally, but AI systems trained in natural language processing can distinguish hype from genuine news, filtering out noise and helping traders stay grounded.

By integrating sentiment analysis into their strategy, traders gain a forward-looking edge—spotting trend shifts before they become visible through price action alone. It's a smarter, more proactive way to make trading decisions in today's fast-moving, emotionally charged markets.

How AI Scans & Analyzes Market Sentiment

AI-powered sentiment analysis transforms unstructured data into actionable trading signals through a multi-step process. It begins with Natural Language Processing (NLP), which allows AI to scan and interpret the emotional tone behind news headlines, earnings transcripts, and social media discussions. Once sentiment is extracted, the system correlates current data with historical market reactions, identifying patterns between similar sentiment spikes and resulting price behavior.

Next, the AI assesses whether the detected sentiment shift is significant enough to influence volatility. It's not just about spotting negative or positive sentiment—it's about measuring the intensity and likelihood of market impact. Finally, if the sentiment aligns with a technically or statistically favorable setup, the AI generates a trading signal, guiding traders toward high-probability opportunities backed by both market psychology and data-driven analysis.

Real-World Example: AI Detecting a Bullish Sentiment Shift

Here's how AI delivers a trading edge in action: It begins by identifying a surge in positive media coverage around a tech company in the days leading up to its earnings announcement. At the same time, sentiment analysis across social platforms like Twitter and Reddit reveals a strong bullish tone, indicating growing retail enthusiasm. Meanwhile, AI picks up on a noticeable uptick in institutional call option activity—a classic sign of growing confidence among professional investors.

Recognizing this alignment across news, sentiment, and options flow, the AI recommends a bullish options setup, such as a call debit spread or a long straddle, to capitalize on the anticipated move. Because the entire analysis happens in real time, traders receive this insight well before the broader market responds—allowing them to position early, with precision.

The Power of AI in Filtering Real vs. Fake News

In today's digital world, financial markets are highly susceptible to misinformation, rumors, and manipulated news. With the rise of social media and instant news cycles, traders often struggle to separate real, impactful events from misleading or exaggerated reports.

AI-powered systems provide a solution by analyzing, cross-referencing, and verifying financial news in real time, ensuring traders act only on reliable, high-confidence data. By filtering market noise, AI prevents traders from making emotion-driven decisions based on false or misleading information.

This section explores how AI detects fake news, protects traders from market manipulation, and ensures data-driven decision-making.

Why Fake News Impacts Trading Decisions

Financial markets react instantly to headlines—often before the underlying facts are confirmed. This creates a major vulnerability for traders: misinformation can trigger emotional decisions, manipulated earnings reports may distort valuations, and social media hype can fuel speculative bubbles around meme stocks.

AI acts as a safeguard in this chaos. By validating news in real time, it filters out false or misleading information and flags only credible, high-impact developments. Instead of getting caught up in noise, traders can focus on fact-based signals. This AI-driven approach not only protects against market manipulation but also sharpens trade timing and improves overall decision quality.

How AI Filters Fake News

AI combats misinformation in trading by assigning a credibility score to news sources, helping distinguish reliable outlets from biased or low-quality ones. This scoring system ensures that traders prioritize information from sources with a strong track record, reducing the influence of clickbait or unverified content.

Next, AI cross-checks breaking news across multiple independent channels to verify its accuracy. If a news item appears on just one platform, it's flagged as potentially unreliable. In contrast, when multiple credible outlets confirm the same story, AI increases its trust rating, making it safer for traders to act on that information.

Finally, AI evaluates the behavior of institutional players—such as insider trades or shifts in large fund positions—and compares them to the news narrative. If the sentiment shown in headlines doesn't match real market reactions or institutional activity, AI detects the discrepancy. This helps traders avoid reacting to hype and instead rely on data-backed market behavior.

Real-World Example: AI Filtering Market Manipulation

A sudden wave of bullish news about a small-cap biotech stock appears across low-credibility websites, triggering retail excitement. However, AI steps in to analyze the situation beyond the headlines.

Upon deeper analysis, the AI system detects no corresponding institutional buying activity or significant volume shifts from credible sources. This lack of confirmation leads the algorithm to flag the move as a high-risk "pump-and-dump" setup—a scenario where misleading hype artificially inflates a stock's price before it crashes.

Rather than following the emotional impulse to buy calls, the AI suggests either avoiding the trade entirely or even considering a short position. By filtering out noise and identifying manipulation, AI helps traders stay grounded in data and avoid emotionally charged traps.

Conclusion:

AI strips away the emotional and manual burdens that often hinder trading performance. With the help of auto-trading bots, trades are executed swiftly and with precision, minimizing human error and maximizing efficiency. These systems work around the clock, tirelessly scanning the market for ideal entry and exit points.

Beyond execution, AI-powered sentiment analysis gives traders an informational edge, identifying high-probability setups based on social sentiment, institutional activity, and real-time news flow. These tools can detect subtle shifts in tone and momentum long before they become obvious to the broader market.

Just as critically, AI acts as a filter for misinformation. By distinguishing between credible news and noise, traders avoid being misled by hype or panic. This data-driven clarity enhances decision-making, reduces risk exposure, and helps traders maintain consistency in the face of volatile market conditions.

CHAPTER 10: THE FUTURE OF AI IN TRADING – WHAT'S NEXT?

Artificial Intelligence is transforming the financial markets at an unprecedented pace, but we are only scratching the surface of what AI can achieve in trading. As machine learning algorithms become more sophisticated and new computing technologies emerge, traders must adapt to stay competitive.

This chapter explores the upcoming innovations in AI-powered trading, including AI-driven hedge funds, quantum computing applications, and the next generation of algorithmic trading strategies. Additionally, it will provide insights on how traders can stay ahead in this evolving landscape through lifelong learning, continuous adaptation, and community engagement.

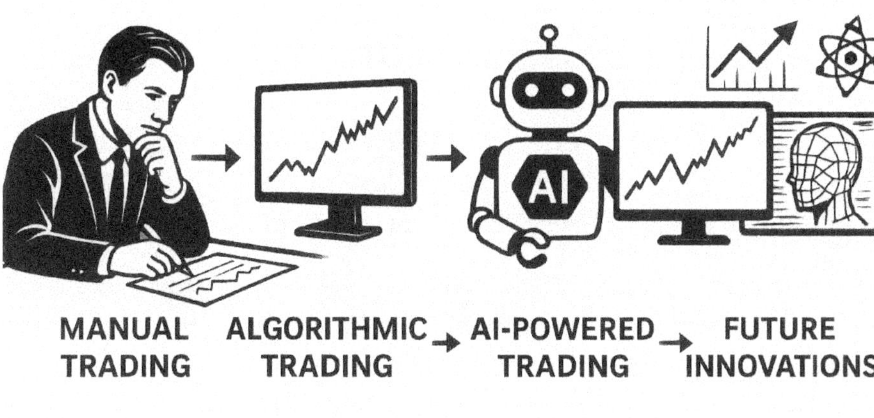

1. Upcoming Innovations in AI & Finance

AI has already transformed high-frequency trading, risk management, and algorithmic execution, but its evolution is far from over. The next decade will see even more sophisticated AI-driven advancements, enabling traders and financial institutions to execute trades faster, smarter, and more efficiently than ever before.

New AI technologies are pushing the boundaries of predictive analytics, automated decision-making, and risk mitigation. From fully autonomous hedge funds to quantum computing-powered financial models, the future of AI in trading is poised to bring unprecedented changes.

This section explores some of the most game-changing AI-driven innovations in finance and how they will impact trading strategies in the years to come.

AI-Driven Hedge Funds: The Next Evolution in Asset Management

AI is not just enhancing individual trading strategies—it is also reshaping entire hedge funds, replacing human-driven investment decision-making with machine learning models and deep learning algorithms. AI-powered hedge funds are proving more adaptive, precise, and efficient than their human counterparts, signaling a major shift in asset management.

By leveraging AI, hedge funds can analyze more data, execute trades faster, and remove emotional bias, resulting in more consistent and scalable returns. Understanding how AI-driven hedge funds operate is crucial for traders looking to stay competitive in an increasingly automated financial landscape.

The Rise of AI-Managed Portfolios

Traditional hedge funds rely on human analysts, economic models, and technical indicators to generate returns. But AI-driven hedge funds are rapidly gaining an edge—often outperforming their human-managed peers.

Thanks to their ability to **process massive volumes of market data in milliseconds**, AI systems spot inefficiencies faster than any human. They **eliminate emotional bias**, ensuring decisions are grounded in pure data, and they **execute high-frequency trades with near-zero latency**, capitalizing on even the smallest price discrepancies.

The result is a new era of portfolio management—faster, smarter, and more precise.

How AI-Powered Hedge Funds Operate

AI-driven hedge funds rely on advanced machine learning models to stay ahead of the market. They use **deep learning algorithms** to uncover non-linear patterns in asset price movements, and **reinforcement learning AI** to adapt trading strategies in real time based on performance feedback.

What sets these funds apart is their ability to integrate **alternative data sources**—from satellite imagery and web traffic to social media sentiment—allowing them to anticipate economic shifts long before traditional financial reports catch up.

Real-World Example: AI Beating Human Hedge Funds

Several hedge funds have already embraced AI-powered decision-making—transforming how strategies are built and executed. **Bridgewater Associates**, the world's largest hedge fund, integrates AI into its models to eliminate human bias. **Renaissance Technologies**, one of the most successful quant funds in history, has relied on AI-driven algorithms to consistently outperform the market for decades.

These examples underscore a clear trend: when investment decisions are guided by data rather than emotion, performance improves—and AI is leading that evolution.

The Impact of Quantum Computing on Trading

The introduction of quantum computing into financial markets will be one of the most revolutionary advancements in the history of trading. While AI has already improved trade execution, risk assessment, and sentiment analysis, quantum computing will push these capabilities to an entirely new level.

Quantum-driven AI will allow traders to process, analyze, and predict market trends at speeds and levels of complexity never before possible. As quantum computing technology matures, traders and institutions that leverage its power early will gain a massive advantage over those still relying on traditional computation.

This section explores what quantum computing is, how it works, and why it will completely reshape trading strategies in the near future.

What is Quantum Computing, and Why Does It Matter?

Quantum computing marks the next frontier in computational power, with the potential to revolutionize trading and financial modeling. Unlike traditional computers that process data in binary (0s and 1s), quantum computers use **qubits**, which can exist in multiple states at once—enabling massively parallel processing.

This breakthrough allows quantum systems to:

⇒ **Analyze thousands of market conditions simultaneously**, identifying optimal strategies in real time
⇒ **Solve complex risk models** in seconds—tasks that would take classical computers days or weeks
⇒ **Optimize portfolio allocation** through multivariable calculations far beyond human or current machine capabilities

As quantum technology evolves, it promises to reshape the future of trading with speed and precision never before imagined.

How Quantum AI Will Transform Trading

Quantum computing is poised to redefine algorithmic trading and financial modeling at their core. It will **enhance options pricing models**, delivering more precise volatility forecasts and fair value estimates. Its unparalleled processing power will **uncover market inefficiencies** faster than any current system, opening new frontiers in arbitrage and predictive analysis.

Most significantly, quantum systems will **transform risk management**—instantly simulating millions of economic scenarios to stress-test portfolios with a depth and speed far beyond today's capabilities.

Real-World Example: Banks & Hedge Funds Investing in Quantum AI

Major financial institutions are already exploring quantum computing to gain a competitive edge. **Goldman Sachs** and **JPMorgan Chase** are actively developing quantum trading models, while **IBM** and **Google** are partnering with financial firms to create quantum-enhanced algorithms. **D-Wave Systems**, a pioneer in the field, has already launched quantum-assisted tools for portfolio optimization.

Though still in its early stages, quantum computing is advancing rapidly—and firms that adopt it early are positioning themselves for a significant strategic advantage in the markets of tomorrow.

2. How to Stay Ahead in AI Trading

With AI-driven trading evolving at an unprecedented pace, traders must embrace a mindset of continuous learning, adaptation, and innovation. Simply understanding today's AI tools and strategies is not enough—staying ahead requires long-term commitment to skill development and networking with other AI-focused traders.

As AI algorithms improve and new computational technologies emerge, the financial landscape will continue to shift dramatically. Traders who fail to adapt risk being left behind, while those who remain at the forefront of AI advancements will consistently outperform the market.

This section explores how traders can future-proof their success by engaging in lifelong learning and building strong AI-focused trading communities.

Lifelong Learning & Continuous Improvement

The most successful traders recognize that financial markets never remain static. Strategies that worked yesterday may become obsolete tomorrow, especially with rapid advancements in AI, deep learning, and big data analytics.

By committing to ongoing education and refinement of their trading strategies, traders ensure they remain competitive, adaptable, and well-prepared for future developments in AI-driven trading.

Why AI Trading Requires Constant Learning

AI represents a fundamental departure from traditional trading methods. Unlike fixed-rule strategies, AI-powered models evolve continuously, adapting to new market conditions and uncovering shifting data patterns in real time. This means that strategies once effective may lose their edge as market dynamics evolve. At the same time, new AI platforms and tools are emerging rapidly, requiring traders to remain agile and well-informed.

Moreover, alternative data sources—such as blockchain analytics and social sentiment—are becoming integral to AI's decision-making process, offering insights far beyond conventional indicators. In this fast-changing landscape, traders who embrace continuous learning, innovation, and research will be best positioned to unlock the full potential of AI and thrive in the markets of tomorrow.

How to Keep Learning & Adapting

To stay ahead in an AI-driven trading landscape, traders must commit to continuous education and adaptation. Engaging in specialized courses—available through platforms like Udemy, Coursera, and MIT Open Courseware—helps build a strong foundation in AI-powered finance. Staying current with research papers, hedge fund insights, and academic publications ensures exposure to the latest strategies and technological developments. Just as important is the regular backtesting of new AI models, which allows traders to refine their approach through practical, data-driven experimentation.

Ultimately, the most successful AI traders are those who view learning as an ongoing process—consistently updating their skills and evolving with the technology.

Building a Community of AI Traders

The Power of Collective Intelligence

Trading is no longer a solitary pursuit—especially in the world of AI. Connecting with other AI-driven traders creates valuable opportunities to exchange strategies, share insights, and collaborate on improving machine learning models. These networks also offer early access to emerging platforms and tools, keeping traders at the forefront of innovation. In a fast-moving, data-intensive environment, collaboration isn't just beneficial—it's a competitive advantage.

Where to Connect with AI Traders

AI trading thrives in collaborative environments, and today's traders have access to a wide range of communities where ideas and strategies are freely exchanged. Online forums and Discord groups—such as r/algo trading—offer real-time discussions on AI techniques and model development. Quantitative trading meetups and global events like the World Quant Finance Conference provide valuable opportunities to connect with AI developers and institutional players. Meanwhile, platforms like QuantConnect and Quantopian foster collaboration by allowing traders to test, refine, and share AI-driven models in a live development environment.

Being active in these communities not only sharpens your skills but also keeps you connected to the forefront of innovation in algorithmic trading.

Real-World Example: AI Traders Sharing Strategies for Higher Returns

In hedge fund communities, traders who collaborate on AI-driven strategies consistently achieve higher returns compared to those working in isolation. Open-source AI trading projects have further demonstrated the power of collective intelligence, enabling participants to fine-tune their models by building on shared insights and experience rather than starting from scratch.

By actively engaging in a network of AI-focused traders, individuals can accelerate their learning curve, refine their strategies more effectively, and significantly boost long-term profitability.

Final Thoughts on The Future of AI in Trading

AI is fundamentally reshaping how traders analyze markets, execute trades, and manage risk. But as this technology continues to evolve, staying ahead means more than just awareness—it requires action. Traders must be willing to adopt emerging innovations early, from quantum trading to advanced deep learning models. Lifelong learning becomes essential, as does staying informed about the latest developments in AI-powered strategies. Just as important is cultivating a strong network—collaborating with other AI-driven traders and developers to share insights and accelerate growth.

The future of trading belongs to those who embrace automation and data-driven decision-making. In a world increasingly shaped by algorithms, those who integrate AI into their trading process will enjoy greater precision, higher efficiency, and a lasting competitive edge.

The next step? Turning AI strategies into a structured, real-world approach. Let's get started.

CASE STUDIES: REAL-WORLD AI TRADING SUCCESS STORIES

Understanding the theory behind AI-powered trading is essential—but the real value emerges when we examine how these concepts are applied in practice. By analyzing how both institutional hedge funds and retail traders use AI for decision-making, risk management, and trade execution, we gain practical insights into what works, what falls short, and how to apply these lessons effectively.

In this chapter, we'll explore three key case studies that demonstrate the transformative impact of AI in trading. First, we'll look at Renaissance Technologies, the hedge fund that pioneered algorithmic and AI-driven strategies. Then, we'll examine how Bridgewater Associates leverages AI for risk management on a global scale. Finally, we'll turn to the world of retail trading to see how individual traders are using AI bots to automate strategies and enhance profitability.

Each case offers a unique perspective on the tools, models, and decision-making frameworks that define successful AI-driven trading today.

1. Renaissance Technologies: The AI-Driven Hedge Fund Giant

<u>Background</u>

Renaissance Technologies is one of the most successful hedge funds in history, founded by Jim Simons, a former mathematician and codebreaker.

Unlike traditional hedge funds that rely on fundamental analysis and economic forecasts, Renaissance Technologies uses pure AI-driven quantitative strategies to manage billions of dollars.

How Renaissance Uses AI for Trading

Renaissance Technologies is renowned for its sophisticated use of AI and machine learning in trading. The firm employs advanced models that continuously process vast datasets to uncover even the slightest market inefficiencies. These AI algorithms analyze historical price action, alternative data streams, and intricate mathematical relationships to forecast short-term price movements with remarkable precision.

Execution speed is a key advantage. Trades are carried out at ultra-high frequencies—often within microseconds—allowing the firm to capture rapid gains from fleeting opportunities that would be invisible to slower systems or human traders.

Key AI Trading Strategies Used by Renaissance

Bridgewater Associates integrates AI across multiple layers of its trading and risk management infrastructure. One key area is **pattern recognition and predictive analytics**, where AI models detect statistical anomalies in market behavior and continuously refine themselves based on which signals historically lead to profitable outcomes.

The firm also leverages **high-frequency trading (HFT)** capabilities, using AI to execute thousands of trades per second—taking advantage of fleeting arbitrage opportunities well before human traders can react.

In addition, Bridgewater employs **automated portfolio rebalancing**, with AI dynamically adjusting position sizes in response to real-time market data.

This ensures that the portfolio remains aligned with its target risk exposure while adapting swiftly to changing conditions.

Lessons for Traders

The experience of leading firms like Renaissance Technologies reveals several key lessons about successful AI-driven trading. First, **AI-powered strategies consistently outperform human intuition**—traders who rely on data, machine learning, and statistical analysis gain a measurable edge over discretionary decision-making.

Second, **rigorous backtesting is non-negotiable**. Before deploying any model live, Renaissance subjects it to extensive simulation across varying market conditions to ensure its robustness and reliability.

Finally, **high-frequency execution at scale is only possible through automation**. Capturing micro-inefficiencies requires the speed, precision, and adaptability that only AI systems can deliver—making them indispensable in today's algorithmic landscape.

2. Bridgewater Associates: AI in Risk Management & Trade Execution

Background

Founded by Ray Dalio, Bridgewater Associates is one of the largest hedge funds in the world, managing over $150 billion in assets. While the firm is known for macro investing strategies, it has increasingly relied on AI-driven risk management and trade execution.

How Bridgewater Uses AI in Trading

Retail traders are increasingly turning to AI bots to level the playing field and enhance their performance. These AI models analyze global economic trends, historical market cycles, and alternative data sources—such as news sentiment and social media signals—to generate actionable investment insights.

Machine learning algorithms are also used to simulate economic downturns, helping traders stress-test their portfolios and **optimize resilience in volatile conditions**. This forward-looking capability allows individual traders to make more informed decisions under pressure.

Finally, AI-powered trade execution systems eliminate the emotional biases that often derail human judgment. By automating entry and exit decisions based on predefined risk-reward criteria, these bots ensure that trades are executed with consistency and discipline—even in fast-moving markets.

Key AI Strategies Used by Bridgewater

Many retail traders are now replicating institutional-grade strategies by adopting AI tools that offer macro-level analysis, risk control, and behavioral optimization. One such approach begins with **AI-based macroeconomic analysis**, where models forecast global market trends using inputs like inflation rates, economic indicators, and geopolitical developments. Based on these forecasts, the AI dynamically adjusts portfolio allocations to align with prevailing macro conditions.

In the area of **risk management**, AI stress-tests portfolios against thousands of simulated economic scenarios, allowing traders to anticipate potential drawdowns and implement protective hedges. When risk exposure exceeds optimal thresholds, the system automatically recommends rebalancing to maintain stability.

Lastly, **AI-driven behavioral insights** play a key role in reducing cognitive biases. By identifying patterns of emotional trading—such as overconfidence or loss aversion—these systems promote disciplined, data-informed decisions that improve long-term outcomes.

<u>Lessons for Traders</u>

Across all levels of trading, AI is proving to be a powerful ally in decision-making and strategy development. In **risk management**, AI-driven backtesting tools allow traders to identify potential market vulnerabilities before they materialize, enabling proactive adjustments. When it comes to **macro trading**, AI's capacity to process and interpret economic data, inflation trends, and global events makes it an invaluable asset for long-term positioning.

Perhaps most importantly, AI fosters **emotion-free trading**—removing the psychological biases that often lead to irrational decisions. By relying on data rather than impulse, traders can operate with greater consistency, discipline, and clarity.

3. Retail Traders: Profiting from AI-Powered Trading Bots

Background

While AI trading has traditionally been dominated by hedge funds, retail traders are now using AI-powered bots to level the playing field. AI trading platforms like Trade Ideas, Option Alpha, and Tickeron allow individual traders to automate trade execution, manage risk, and optimize options strategies.

How Retail Traders Use AI Bots

Retail traders are increasingly harnessing AI to automate and refine their trading strategies. **Automated options trading bots** now execute strategies like credit spreads, iron condors, and covered calls based on real-time market conditions—removing guesswork and improving consistency. At the same time, **AI-powered sentiment analysis tools** scan financial news and social media feeds to detect early signs of market shifts, allowing traders to react ahead of broader trends.

To ensure reliability, many traders rely on **algorithmic backtesting** to validate AI-generated trade signals before execution. This approach blends automation with disciplined verification—helping retail investors compete more confidently in complex markets.

Key AI Strategies Used by Retail Traders

Retail traders are adopting increasingly advanced AI strategies to compete with institutional-level precision. One popular approach is **AI-optimized covered calls**, where the system selects stocks with low implied volatility and a high probability of success. Execution is automated, allowing traders to generate steady, passive income through a disciplined covered call cycle.

For more active strategies, **AI-powered scalping and day trading bots** scan thousands of stocks per second, identifying short-term momentum opportunities. These bots instantly enter and exit positions based on real-time trend analysis, eliminating human delay and maximizing efficiency.

Another rising trend is **sentiment-based trading**. Here, AI models analyze vast volumes of social media posts, earnings call transcripts, and financial headlines to detect subtle shifts in market mood. These insights allow traders to anticipate breakouts or reversals—often before the broader market has time to react.

<u>Lessons for Traders</u>

AI is empowering retail traders like never before—making sophisticated strategies more accessible and execution more efficient. **AI-powered bots** automate repetitive, time-consuming tasks, allowing traders to focus on refining their strategy rather than managing each trade manually. Through **backtesting**, traders can validate AI-generated signals against historical data, reducing risk and building confidence before going live.

Perhaps most significantly, AI is **leveling the playing field**. What was once the domain of hedge funds and quant firms is now within reach for individual traders—enabling them to compete using the same data-driven tools and techniques as institutional players.

Final Thoughts on AI-Powered Trading Success

These case studies clearly demonstrate how AI is reshaping trading across the spectrum—from multi-billion-dollar hedge funds to individual retail traders. Despite the differences in scale, the same core principles emerge: **data-driven decision-making consistently outperforms intuition**, **AI**

reduces emotional bias and enhances risk control, and **automated execution boosts both efficiency and profit potential**.

For traders ready to embrace this shift, the path forward is clear: apply the strategies, tools, and insights explored in these case studies to build a smarter, more disciplined trading routine.

The AI revolution in trading isn't coming—it's already here. The only question is: are you ready to take part?

CONCLUSION & FINAL RESOURCES

The rise of AI in options trading is not just a trend—it's a fundamental shift in how traders analyze data, execute trades, and manage risk. Throughout this book, we have explored how AI enhances trading strategies, automates decision-making, and minimizes risk exposure.

As financial markets continue to evolve, traders who embrace AI and automation will maintain a significant edge over those who rely solely on traditional methods. However, mastering AI-powered trading is not a one-time event—it's a continuous journey of learning, adapting, and optimizing strategies.

This final chapter will provide a recap of the key concepts covered in this book, offer practical advice on integrating AI into your daily trading routine, and share additional resources to help you continue your growth as an AI trader.

The Road to Becoming an AI Trader

Recap of Key Concepts

We've covered a lot of ground in this book, from understanding AI's role in financial markets to implementing AI-enhanced options trading strategies. Below is a quick recap of the core concepts that every AI trader should master:

1. **Understanding AI in Trading**

AI and machine learning are transforming every facet of trading—from how markets are analyzed to how trades are executed and risks are managed. Today's traders can harness predictive analytics, sentiment analysis, and automated execution to refine their strategies, improve timing, and operate with greater precision. The result is a more agile, intelligent approach to trading—driven by data, not guesswork.

2. **Options Trading Fundamentals**

Options trading provides a powerful combination of flexibility, leverage, and risk management—making it a versatile tool for traders at all levels. To use it effectively, however, it's essential to master the fundamentals. Understanding how calls and puts work, how to evaluate strike prices and expiration dates, and how to interpret the Greeks is crucial for building strategies that are both informed and resilient.

3. **AI-Powered Trading Strategies**

AI is reshaping how traders approach strategy—especially in areas like trend following, volatility-based setups, and hedging. Advanced models can uncover hidden market patterns that escape traditional analysis, optimize entry and exit points with greater precision, and automate risk management to respond dynamically to real-time conditions. The result is a smarter, faster, and more adaptive way to trade in any market environment.

4. **Automating Your Trading Routine**

AI-driven bots are redefining the trading workflow by executing trades, managing open positions, and tracking market sentiment in real time. These systems bring speed, consistency, and data awareness to every stage of the trading process. Platforms like Trade Ideas, Tickeron, and Option Alpha make it easier than ever for traders to integrate AI tools into their daily routine—bridging the gap between strategy and execution with intelligent automation.

5. **The Future of AI in Trading**

The next wave of AI innovation is already taking shape—driven by developments like fully autonomous hedge funds, quantum computing applied to trading, and adaptive learning models that evolve in real time. As these technologies mature, they will redefine what's possible in the markets. Traders who stay ahead of these advancements and integrate them into their strategies will be best positioned to maintain a lasting edge in an increasingly data-driven financial landscape.

These core concepts form the foundation of AI-powered trading success, but the real challenge is turning knowledge into action.

How to Integrate AI into Your Daily Trading

Mastering AI-powered trading requires more than theoretical understanding—it demands practical application and ongoing adaptation. Here's how to seamlessly integrate AI into your trading routine:

1. **Start Small with AI-Assisted Trading**

If you're new to AI-driven strategies, resist the urge to jump straight into full automation. Begin by using AI to screen markets, generate trade signals, and manage risk. AI-powered tools can help you set intelligent stop-loss levels and control position sizing. Before risking real capital, test these strategies in a paper trading environment to validate performance under live conditions.

2. **Automate Repetitive Tasks to Boost Efficiency**

One of AI's greatest strengths is its ability to handle time-consuming, repetitive tasks. Let your AI tools scan thousands of options contracts for high-probability setups, automate covered call and cash-secured put strategies, and monitor real-time sentiment or institutional order flow. By automating the operational side, you free up time and energy to focus on strategic decision-making.

3. **Backtest and Continuously Optimize Your Models**

The edge in AI trading comes from refinement. Run backtest using historical data across different market environments to evaluate performance. Adjust machine learning parameters based on outcomes, and consider integrating alternative data—such as earnings call transcripts or social sentiment—to enhance your model's predictive power.

4. **Stay Current with AI Trading Innovations**

AI is a fast-moving field. To stay ahead, immerse yourself in the latest research, follow thought leaders in AI and finance, and engage with trading communities focused on machine learning. Experiment regularly with new tools and platforms—constant evolution is key to long-term success.

In the end, the most successful AI traders aren't those who set it and forget it—they're the ones who adapt, refine, and consistently improve. The technology is powerful, but it's your commitment to learning and iteration that turns it into lasting edge.

Additional Resources for AI Trading Mastery

When it comes to AI-powered trading, choosing the right tools and staying connected with like-minded traders can make a significant difference. Several platforms have emerged as leaders in this space. Trade Ideas, for example, is highly regarded for its real-time AI stock and options scanning, making it a favorite among short-term traders. Tickeron offers AI-generated trade signals and comprehensive portfolio analysis, while Option Alpha provides fully automated bots that execute predefined options strategies. For those interested in building custom algorithms, QuantConnect stands out as a robust platform. Meanwhile, Kaggle and the now-archived Quantopian remain influential communities for quantitative strategy development and AI experimentation.

Beyond platforms, the right community can accelerate your learning and keep you on the cutting edge. The subreddit r/algotrading is one of the largest and most active forums dedicated to algorithmic and AI-based trading. QuantConnect's own community offers deep collaboration among developers building AI trading models. Many traders also join specialized Discord servers where real-time discussions, code sharing, and AI trade ideas are exchanged daily. For those seeking direct mentorship or industry connections, events like the World Quant Finance Conference and various AI trading hackathons provide unmatched opportunities to engage with professionals at the forefront of finance and technology.

By immersing yourself in these tools, communities, and mentorship networks, you'll not only enhance your technical skills but also position yourself to thrive in the evolving world of AI-driven trading.

Final Thoughts: The Future Belongs to AI Traders

The integration of AI into options trading isn't just a step forward—it's a complete transformation. Those who embrace this technology gain a significant edge, unlocking the ability to analyze data with a speed and depth far beyond human capability. They automate trade execution and risk management, ensuring greater consistency and fewer emotional errors. They respond to market shifts with adaptive machine learning models that evolve alongside the markets themselves.

Yet, it's important to remember that the power of AI lies not only in its algorithms but in the mindset of the trader who uses them. Success in this new era doesn't come from technology alone—it's rooted in continuous learning, disciplined execution, and the willingness to evolve.

The financial markets of tomorrow will belong to those who can harness AI's full potential. So ask yourself: are you ready to be one of them?

The journey doesn't stop here. Keep learning, keep refining your approach, and continue trading smarter with the intelligence of AI by your side.

www.ingramcontent.com/pod-product-compliance
Lightning Source LLC
Chambersburg PA
CBHW050527240926
51846CB00003B/727
9783691043679